Internal Dialogue

A BUSY WRITER'S GUIDE

Marcy Kennedy

Tongue Untied Communications
ONTARIO, CANADA

Marcy Kennedy
marcykennedy@gmail.com
www.marcykennedy.com

Book Layout ©2013 BookDesignTemplates.com
Edited by Chris J. Saylor
Cover Design by Melinda VanLone

Internal Dialogue/ Marcy Kennedy —1st ed.
ISBN 978-1-988069-01-2

Contents

Why a Busy Writer's Guide?

Every "how to become a better writer" list includes studying craft. Years ago, as a new writer, I took that advice to heart, but found that many craft books didn't give me the detailed, in-the-trenches coverage of a topic I wanted. They included a lot of beautifully written prose and theory without explaining how to practically apply the principles, or they gave numerous examples but didn't explain how to replicate those concepts in my own work.

I ended up buying three or four books on the same topic to understand it fully and get the balance of theory and practice I was looking for. I spent more time studying craft than writing, and all the exercises in the books seemed to take me away from my story rather than helping me work directly on it. For the modern writer who also needs to blog and be on social media, who might be juggling a day job, and who still wants time to see their family or friends, that's a problem. Do you know anyone who doesn't have more commitments than they're able to handle already without adding "study the writing craft" on top of it?

We're busy. We're tired. We're overworked. We love writing, but often wonder if it's worth the sacrifices we're making for it. We know we're headed down the fast track to burning out, but don't know what we can do differently.

I wrote *The Busy Writer's Guide* series to help you fast-track the learning process. I felt that writers needed a fluff-free guide that would give them the detailed coverage of a topic they required while also respecting their time. I want you to be able to spend the majority of your writing time actually writing, so that you can set aside your computer and enjoy the people and experiences that make life worth living.

Each *Busy Writer's Guide* is intended to serve as an accelerated master's class in a topic. I'll give you enough theory so that you can understand why things work and why they don't, but also enough examples to see how that theory looks in practice. I'll also provide tips and exercises to help you take it to the pages of your own story with an editor's-eye view.

My goal is for you to come away a stronger writer, with a stronger piece of work, than when you came in.

So let's get started...

CHAPTER ONE

What Is Internal Dialogue?

Have you ever had one of those conversations (a.k.a. arguments) where you realize twenty minutes in that you're either talking about different things or you're actually in agreement but you were confused because you were both expressing your opinion differently? I don't want our study of internal dialogue to end up that way, so I want to clarify terms first.

Throughout this book, I'll be using *internal dialogue* as synonymous with *internal monologue, interior monologue, inner monologue, interior dialogue,* and *inner dialogue*, so don't get stuck on terminology. What we're looking at is the concept behind the terms. (If you'd like to break down the terminology, please see Appendix A: Internal Dialogue, Internal Monologue, Soliloquy, and Other Terms.)

Internal dialogue is one of the most powerful tools in a fiction writer's arsenal. It's an advantage we have over TV and movie script writers and playwrights. What we lose by not having physical scenery and actors' facial expressions and movement playing out in front of the audience, we more than gain back in internal dialogue. So we need to make the best possible use of it.

First, though, we need to make sure we're clear on what we mean by *internal dialogue* because being able to write strong internal dialogue depends in part on understanding exactly what it is—and what it *isn't*.

The Difference Between Internal Dialogue and Narration

The simplest definition is that internal dialogue is what your character is thinking.

However, because the definition is so simple, a lot of writers get confused about the difference between the character thinking naturally to themselves and a character narrating for the benefit of the reader. Internal dialogue is not the same as narration.

Internal dialogue is the conversation we have with ourselves, the running commentary inside our heads about our day. It isn't meant for anyone else to hear. It's private. Most of us would be horrified if these thoughts were played aloud because it's where our deepest fears, self-recriminations, and personal lies hide.

Narration is when the person telling the story (the narrator) speaks directly to the reader. It's meant to be heard. Narration can be good or bad, but it's never internal dialogue. You can find examples of narration in the first chapter of Lemony Snicket's *The Bad Beginning* and Pittacus Lore's *I Am Number Four*.

The opening to J.R.R. Tolkien's *The Fellowship of the Ring* is also narration. Take a look at how it starts.

> This book is largely concerned with Hobbits, and from its pages a reader may discover much of their character and a little of their history.

The narrator of the book is directly addressing the reader with this opening. He's not thinking to himself.

How much internal dialogue vs. narration you use depends on what point of view (POV) you're writing in, and the best way to see the difference is to choose three books in the same genre but written in the different POVs and make notes on how often and in what balance they use both.

Omniscient POV uses less internal dialogue than does third-person POV because we're more distant from the characters. The omniscient narrator may, at times, speak more directly to the reader.

If you're writing in third-person POV, you need to have predominantly internal dialogue if you want readers to connect emotionally with your characters. If you're writing in a deep, intimate third-person POV, you'll be using internal dialogue almost exclusively.

First-person POV is the point of view that most often balances internal dialogue with narration. Due to the nature of the way the story is told, it feels like the point-of-view character is talking to us, the reader. They're telling us a story, and during that story, they share with us some of the private, personal thoughts that they'd never be able to share with anyone they know.

An Example from *While You Were Sleeping*

The movie *While You Were Sleeping* uses both internal dialogue and narration, so it's a great way to point out how they're different. (If you don't own the movie, search for it on YouTube or Netflix and watch until the Christmas tree goes through the window.)

The movie starts with a voice-over as we see a little girl and her father on a bridge, with the sun setting in the background.

Lucy, the main character, is talking directly to us at this point. It's narration. This is what we want to avoid when we're trying to write internal dialogue. We don't want it to feel like the main character is talking at us. It tends to come across like a lecture, and lectures are boring. And, more importantly for the issue at hand, it's not internal dialogue.

Instead, internal dialogue should feel like we're eavesdropping on our character's thoughts to herself.

A little later in the movie, we see Lucy trying to haul a Christmas tree through her window into her upper-floor apartment. She rants to herself about how they wouldn't deliver the tree despite the price, and how even the Chinese restaurant brings the food to your door.

In a novel, this would have been given to the reader as Lucy's thoughts. That is internal dialogue, and it's amazing when done well.

The Two Unbreakable Rules of Internal Dialogue

When it comes to writing, I normally don't like to talk about "rules" because I find we writers get caught up in the terminology of "rules" and suddenly we start wanting to be rule breakers or we talk about knowing when to break the rules. We get so caught up in the terminology that the focus shifts from what it should be on—making our writing the best it can be. Because of that, I normally like to talk about guidelines or best practices—things that are true 99% of the time, but that allow for some flexibility and exceptions depending on the story's needs.

Occasionally, however, we do run into actual writing rules. Actual writing *rules* shouldn't be broken. Ever. I'll make sure that I point these out to you, and that I let you know when what I'm explaining is a guideline instead. If I call something a rule, please understand that breaking it will come with negative consequences for your writing.

Rule #1 – Use internal dialogue only for the point-of-view character...

...unless you're writing in omniscient POV, where the narrator knows all. Outside of omniscient POV, if you introduce internal dialogue for a non-POV character, it's head-hopping, one of the worst point-of-view sins. (If you aren't sure what I mean by *head-hopping*, read Appendix B: Head-Hopping vs. Omniscient POV.)

Rule #2 – Only share thoughts that advance the story.

We don't need to hear every passing thought that flits through your character's head. We do need to hear the important ones. Internal dialogue must be relevant to your plot.

But If It Follows These Rules, Does That Mean It's Good?

If your internal dialogue follows these two rules, it still needs to pass the three question test in order to be deemed *good* internal dialogue. If it fails, you should either rewrite it or delete it.

Question #1 - Would my character think about this?

Do you normally mull over the color of your carpet? I don't. I also don't think about the color of my best friend's hair (because I've seen it so many times). I don't think about the sound my truck makes or even what route to take to get home.

If your character doesn't care about it, they won't think about it. If your character wouldn't think about it, it's a point-of-view error. You can't try to sneak in information through internal dialogue, no matter how important you think it is. There are better ways to introduce necessary information than resorting to point-of-view errors.

Question #2 - Is this the way they'd think it?

If your internal dialogue passes the first test, you still need to ask if they'd think about it in the way you've written it.

Let's say I would be thinking about my truck because it starts to make a strange noise while I'm driving home. I'm likely to worry about whether I'm going to get stranded on the side of the road in the dark or about where we'll get the money for repairs if something is wrong. I might wonder if I missed a recall notice. If you asked me to describe the noise, I'd phrase it in a way that relates it to something I'm familiar with. For example, maybe it sounds like the time I tried to drag a heavy table across the floor. Maybe it sounds like the time a pocketful of change ended up in the dryer.

If my dad is driving my truck and hears a strange noise, he's going to describe it in words I'd never think of (a rattle, a grind, a whine, a screech), and he's going to think about what the causes could be. He knows the parts of an engine or the braking system.

But it goes further than this. What tone would they use in this situation? If you've already read *Dialogue: A Busy Writer's Guide*, all those questions we asked to help make dialogue unique to your characters apply to internal dialogue as well.

Question #3 - Would they be thinking this <u>now</u>?

Context is everything. On a normal day, I might hear that noise and think about it. If a man in the passenger seat has a gun pointed at me, I'm not going to think about that noise unless I can leverage it to escape.

So now that we're clear on *what* internal dialogue is, we should make sure we know *why* it's important to fiction writing.

The Value of Internal Dialogue in Fiction

Understanding *why* something is important to our writing lays the foundation for bettering our writing because it acts as a measuring post. When we know why we should do something and what benefit we're supposed to gain by doing it, it helps us recognize when we're not receiving that benefit. In other words, if our internal dialogue isn't providing one of these benefits, then we're either doing it wrong or we've tried to include it in a spot where it doesn't belong.

With that in mind, let's look at the main reasons why internal dialogue is important to include in our fiction.

Internal dialogue replicates real life.

When we write, we want our work to feel realistic and authentic (even if it's set on a strange planet, includes magic, or has dragons living next door to our banker). We want it to feel like the people could have lived and would have done the things we describe them doing. In our lives, we're always thinking to ourselves—noticing things happening around us, trying to solve problems, giving ourselves a pep talk or a dressing down. If we want our characters to feel real, we need to have them do the same thing.

Internal dialogue creates a deeper connection between the reader and the characters.

For a reader to invest their time in our story, they need to care what happens. Internal dialogue is one of the tools at our disposal to make them care because it creates an intimate connection between the reader and the point-of-view character. We hear their thoughts in the same way we hear our own, and that allows us, as readers, to share their feelings and concerns, experiencing them as our own. We also get to know them better, and they become more real to us because of it.

Internal dialogue helps control the pacing in our fiction.

I once heard the analogy that pacing in fiction is like creating the perfect rollercoaster ride. If you had a rollercoaster that only went up, only went down in one continuous drop for three minutes, or stayed completely level the whole time, no one would ride it. A good rollercoaster needs the anticipation of the rise, the heart-in-the-throat drops, and the shocking loops and twists. Good fiction needs the same. If your entire book was composed of high-speed action scenes, your reader would soon grow as bored as if your whole book was a character sitting in their room and thinking. You need the internal dialogue to create the anticipation for the action, allow the reader to breathe, and build them up for the next drop.

Internal dialogue minimizes confusion by revealing motivations.

The heart of fiction is the *why*. Why is a character acting the way they are? Why do they want to reach their goal so badly that they're willing to suffer the possible consequences? When those motivations aren't clear to the reader, the reader ends up either feeling confused or feeling less engaged with the story. When the reader doesn't know or understand a character's motivations, their actions seem random and are, therefore, less believable. Before our characters act, it needs to be clear what their plan is and why they're pursuing that course of action.

Internal dialogue conveys information that can't be given any other way.

If, for example, you have a character who needs to deceive everyone around them, you'll have them acting one way and thinking another. Another example of this is backstory that influences who our characters are and why (there's that word again) they act the way they do. They might not think that events in their past are influencing them, so they'd have no reason to talk about it with anyone else, but we can make the reader aware of it through their thoughts.

Internal dialogue contributes to our stories in a multitude of subtle ways as well—and those will become clearer later on in this book—but I hope that you now have a better understanding of why we, as writers, need to go to all the trouble of creating fantastic internal dialogue.

TAKE IT TO THE PAGE

If you're working on your first draft, or if you're reading this book to get a working knowledge of the topic but aren't ready yet to work on revising/editing your book based on what you're learning, skip the Take It to the Page section at the end of each chapter. When you're ready to start re-writes/edits, you can always come back to them.

To become stronger writers, we need to both study and practice. My goal for my *Busy Writer's Guides* is to help you fast-track the learning process.

Sometimes this means I'll also suggest other valuable resources the way I did when I recommended *The Emotion Thesaurus* in *Showing and Telling in Fiction: A Busy Writer's Guide*. Sometimes it means I'll recommend a study technique that involves reading great stories. We can learn a lot from carefully observing how other talented writers achieve certain techniques.

I try to make these additional recommendations sparingly because I want to respect your limited time.

Consequently, if you're already comfortable with the difference between narration and internal dialogue and what balance of the two you need in your genre and point of view, then you can skip this recommendation.

If you're new to writing or still struggling with narration vs. internal dialogue and finding the balance of internal dialogue within your book, this extra study (think of it like extra credit) is for you.

In Chapter One, I said one of the best ways to understand the difference between narration and internal dialogue, and to see the balance between the two in different points of view, was to study books in the same genre that use different points of view. That's great if you have a lot of time. If you don't, there's a quick version you can use that targets your needs specifically.

Step 1 – Identify what genre and point of view you're writing in. Pick three published books you love that match both your genre and point of view. These should be books so good you wish you'd written them.

Step 2 – Because this is the quick version, pick a chapter or two from each book and read it, marking/making note of which passages are internal dialogue, which are narration, and which are unclear. (Remember, you're only looking at internal dialogue or narration, so you're not marking things like dialogue or action.)

Some ebook readers have a function for highlighting/making notes. If you have a paper version of the book, you could scan or photocopy the chapter you want to study. This allows you to actually highlight and make notes right on to the physical pages. (Some of you might be comfortable with writing directly in your books, too.)

Step 3 – When you finish, look for patterns. How much internal dialogue did the writers use compared to how much narration? How much internal dialogue compared to other elements (e.g., dialogue, action, description) did the author use?

Step 4 – Take a chapter from your current work in progress and highlight it in the same way. Compare it to the chapters from the published books. Do you see a difference in the patterns? This is a great way to identify weaknesses in your internal dialogue use compared to the successful books in your genre.

CHAPTER TWO

Direct vs. Indirect Internal Dialogue

When it comes to internal dialogue, the most common question is "how do I format it?" It's easier than you think. I'm going to break it down for you in the next chapter, but first we need to cover the difference between direct and indirect internal dialogue. Much of the confusion around formatting happens because writers don't realize that internal dialogue comes in two types.

Indirect internal dialogue gives the reader an idea of the point-of-view character's thoughts, but not the exact words they're thinking.

Direct internal dialogue gives the reader the exact words that the point-of-view character is thinking. It's written in first person and present tense, regardless of the person and tense of the rest of the story.

Direct vs. indirect internal dialogue isn't a case of good vs. evil. Many authors use both within the same story, and when you're writing in deep POV, the line between the two is often fuzzy.

Under the umbrella of indirect internal dialogue, however, you do find good and bad. Indirect internal dialogue can easily turn into telling (rather than showing). If you don't know what I mean by showing and telling, please read Appendix C before continuing. You can also pick up a copy of my book *Showing and Telling in Fiction* for in-depth coverage.

To clarify what I mean, I'm going to walk you through some examples of bad indirect internal dialogue, good indirect internal dialogue, and direct internal dialogue.

For our first example, let's say we have a woman whose husband comes home, supposedly straight from work, but he smells strange, like lilies. You want to have her think about that and wonder why he smells like lilies, where he could have been to smell like lilies.

Keep in mind as I show you how this could be written that I'm showing you only a few possible ways to express this idea. How you personally might chose to express this idea as direct or indirect dialogue might not be the same as how I've chosen to do it. What I want you to pay attention to are the differences between the types of internal dialogue. That's the important part, and I'll point them out.

BAD Indirect Internal Dialogue:

> She wondered where he'd been that he came home smelling like lilies. She couldn't think of anywhere that smelled like that except a funeral parlor filled with flower arrangements.

In this example, we, the writers, have stepped between the character and the reader, and we're acting like a filter. Instead of allowing the reader access to the inside of the character and showing the reader what's going on behind the curtain (allowing the character to act as the filter), we're telling them what's going on.

A couple of things signal that this could be bad indirect internal dialogue. The first is the word *wondered*. Both the words *wondered* and *realized* can be an indicator that you're telling the reader the point-of-view character is realizing or wondering rather than showing them realize or showing them wonder.

Another red flag is the phrase *she couldn't think of*. A phrase like this doesn't always indicate bad indirect internal dialogue, but it means we should take a closer look. It suggests that we're telling the reader what our character couldn't do rather than showing our character trying and failing to do it.

Bad indirect internal dialogue has a distancing effect. It strips away the character's personality, making it lifeless. It's also unnecessary to write it this way. If we don't want to use direct internal dialogue, we have another option—turn it into good indirect internal dialogue.

Turning this into good indirect internal dialogue can be simple. All we need to do is rephrase it to remove the word *wondered* and make the event immediate rather than secondhand.

GOOD Indirect Internal Dialogue:

> The stench of lilies clung to his clothes and hair. It seemed like a smell she should recognize, one she knew. The idea bounced around in her mind the same as a word that wouldn't come off the tip of her tongue when she needed it. It was too natural to be perfume. It didn't smell like any place they regularly went.
>
> She shuddered. *Death.* He smelled like death, like a funeral parlor crowded with flower arrangements and a corpse.

A bit of direct internal dialogue sneaked into this paragraph with the word *death* (which I italicized). As I mentioned in the opening to this chapter, you'll often need to interweave direct and indirect internal dialogue for the best results.

What I want you to pay attention to here, though, is how removing the crutch of *wondered* pushes us to bring this internal dialogue to life for the reader. When we can't fall back on *wondered,* we have to think about the contents of what she was wondering and show her going through the process.

Those details are what differentiate good indirect internal dialogue from bad indirect internal dialogue. When we tell the reader that the character wondered something, it leaves too much room for misinterpretation and confusion. What if the reader doesn't guess correctly about what the character was wondering?

When you're trying to decide whether you've written good or bad indirect internal dialogue, ask yourself if it's clear what your character is thinking. The key to avoiding bad indirect internal dialogue is to ensure that we're giving enough details that the reader knows what's going on.

Before I show you an example of direct internal dialogue, I want to show you another version of good indirect internal dialogue. The previous example was from a more distant, limited third-person point of view. (In other words, we were hearing the story told from the perspective of a single character, but we weren't as tightly connected to her as we could have been.) The following example is indirect internal dialogue from a close third-person point of view, which is also known as writing in deep POV.

GOOD Indirect Internal Dialogue:

> The suffocating stench of lilies clung to his clothes and hair, out of place among his usual coming-home-from-work scents of antiseptic soap and coffee.
>
> She slowly pulled away from his hug. Shivers traced over her arms. She knew that smell. Not perfume. It was

too natural for that, but it also wasn't an everyday odor. She wouldn't expect to run into it at the grocery store. Or the bank, either. It was rare. Heavy, warm, and sad.

Her breath tripped in her throat, and she stepped back. He smelled like death, like a corpse smothered in flower arrangements at a funeral parlor. The last time she'd smelled it was standing next to her mother's coffin, saying goodbye.

In this example, we hear her essentially saying to herself *I should recognize that smell*, and working through where she remembers it from in her own words.

Look at the specific word choices she makes—*suffocating, clung, death*. She associates the fragrance of lilies with grief and death. Those are her words. That's what would have gone through her head.

However, it's not direct internal dialogue because it's still written in past tense and third person. I wanted to show you this example before giving you an example of direct internal dialogue because it's important to see how blurry the line between direct and indirect internal dialogue can be when you're writing from a deep point of view.

Direct Internal Dialogue:

The suffocating stench of lilies clung to his clothes and hair, out of place among his usual coming-home-from-work scents of antiseptic soap and coffee.

She slowly pulled away from his hug. Shivers traced over her arms. *I know that smell. I should know that smell.*

Not perfume. It was too natural for that, but it also wasn't an everyday odor. She wouldn't expect to run into it at the grocery store. Or the bank, either. It was rare. Heavy, warm, and sad.

Her breath tripped in her throat, and she stepped back. *He smells like death, like a corpse smothered in flowers at a funeral parlor.* The last time she'd smelled that scent was standing next to her mother's coffin, saying goodbye.

You'll notice again that this weaves indirect and direct internal dialogue together. The direct internal dialogue is in present tense, is in first person, and is italicized.

The key to distinguishing between direct and indirect internal dialogue is that simple.

Is it in first person, present tense?

Yes – Then it's direct internal dialogue.

No – Then it's indirect internal dialogue.

Because this is an important concept, I'm going to give you another set of examples, starting off with bad indirect internal dialogue again.

BAD Indirect Internal Dialogue:

Janie watched Frank hunched over the map and realized she'd never convince him to take the mountain path without a dang good reason. She needed him to take that mountain path or all the plans she'd made with Jake would be worth nothing. She had to convince Frank that the shelter provided by the caves outweighed the numerous disadvantages.

In this case, it's clear what the character is thinking. Janie knows Frank isn't going to go the way she wants him to and that will ruin all her plans.

What makes this bad indirect internal dialogue again is how far we're being held from the point-of-view character (Janie). We've told the reader she realized something rather than showing her realizing it. In other words, we're summarizing for the reader when we should be showing it happen in real time.

Then we're stating the goal and stakes. It's good to use internal dialogue to reveal our characters' goals and motivations, but we need to do it in the right way—a way that brings it to life for the reader. Those goals, motivations, and stakes should come across naturally as the character thinks about their situation rather than in a way that feels like the author is intruding to make sure the reader "gets it."

GOOD Indirect Internal Dialogue:

> Frank hunched over the map, using his fingers to trace out the different options for their escape route. His hand never even veered in the direction of the mountain path. The mountains provided too many places for ambush, not to mention the bears and fewer chances at restocking along the way.
>
> Janie gnawed on her bottom lip. Frank was practical. She could take advantage of that by giving him a good enough reason to take the mountain path anyway.
>
> She laid her hand on top of the massive pile of gear. "If we carry all this, it's going to slow us down. We could leave at least half of it behind if we used the Danbury Ridge caves instead. And we'd be able to have a fire without lightin' ourselves up like a lighthouse beacon."

Let's look at this again, going into a deeper POV but still using indirect internal dialogue.

GOOD Indirect Internal Dialogue:

> Frank hunched over the map, using his fingers to trace out the different options for their escape route. His hand never even veered in the direction of the mountain path.

Too many places for ambush in the mountains. Too many bears. No chance to restock. He didn't need to list the reasons out loud for her to know them. In any other situation, she would have agreed with him.

But Jake gave her one job—make sure Frank takes the mountain path.

She could do this. What one overwhelming advantage was there to taking that path over sticking to the plains? She bit her bottom lip. The caves.

She laid her hand on top of the massive pile of gear. "If we carry all this, it's going to slow us down. We could leave at least half of it behind if we used the Danbury Ridge caves instead. And we'd be able to have a fire without lightin' ourselves up like a lighthouse beacon."

Now I'll show you the same example rewritten as direct internal dialogue. The direct internal dialogue is italicized.

Direct Internal Dialogue:

Frank hunched over the map, using his fingers to trace out the different options for their escape route. His hand never even veered in the direction of the mountain path.

Too many places for ambush in the mountains. Too many bears. No chance to restock. He didn't need to list the reasons out loud for her to know them. In any other situation, she would have agreed with him.

But Jake gave her one job—make sure Frank takes the mountain path.

She scrubbed a hand under the brim of her hat. *I can do this. What one overwhelming advantage is there to taking that path over sticking to the plains?* She bit her bottom lip. *The caves.*

She laid her hand on top of the massive pile of gear. "If we carry all this, it's going to slow us down. We could leave at least half of it behind if we used the Danbury Ridge caves instead. And we'd be able to have a fire without lightin' ourselves up like a lighthouse beacon."

Let me give you one more example because I want you to see how the difference between indirect and direct internal dialogue can sometimes be minor.

Remember not to get caught up in the exact phrases I use. Instead, pay attention to the big-picture differences in the passages. This time I'm only going to show you good indirect internal dialogue compared to direct internal dialogue. I'll underline the internal dialogue in both examples.

Indirect Internal Dialogue:

A flush crept up the waitress's neck, and she blinked rapidly. Emily mouthed the words *I'm sorry*, but couldn't be sure if she noticed. The girl spun on her heel and scurried away.

Emily glared at Jared. "That was cruel."

"Lighten up." A smirk twisted his lips in a way she used to find endearing. "I was just teasing her."

Emily pushed her food away and closed her eyes. <u>Jerk. She never should have married him. But she'd taken vows and now she had no way out...and he knew it as well as she did.</u>

Direct Internal Dialogue:

A flush crept up the waitress's neck, and she blinked rapidly. Emily mouthed the words *I'm sorry*, but couldn't be sure if she noticed. The girl spun on her heel and scurried away.

She glared at Jared. "That was cruel."

"Lighten up." A smirk twisted his lips in a way she used to find endearing. "I was just teasing her."

Emily pushed her food away and closed her eyes. *Jerk. I never should have married you. But I took vows and now I have no way out...and you know it as well as I do.*

The difference between the two types of internal dialogue in this example is only in the person and tense.

Both indirect and direct internal dialogue are fine to use. The amount of each you include depends on your personal writing voice and the story you're writing.

The important thing to take away from this chapter is this— make sure that you're writing internal dialogue that gives a clear picture of the point-of-view character's thoughts. Vague internal dialogue doesn't move the story forward and can leave the reader confused.

Whether you're writing indirect or direct internal dialogue can also play a role in how you format it, which is what we're going to look at in the next chapter.

Before we move on, there are two more questions we need to answer concerning direct and indirect internal dialogue.

How Do We Know If We're Using Too Much Direct Internal Dialogue?

Direct internal dialogue comes with the advantages of showcasing the character's voice and adding a sense of immediacy. It also comes with risks. It adds emphasis to internal dialogue and draws the reader's attention to it. The internal dialogue that you make direct automatically gains importance. This is especially true when you add italics or thought tags to the internal dialogue.

Because direct internal dialogue stands out, it's better to save it for the most important thoughts only and to use good indirect internal dialogue for the rest. If you're writing in deep POV in third person, you might choose not to use direct internal dialogue at all.

What If I'm Already Writing in Present Tense or in First Person? How Do I Handle Direct Internal Dialogue Then?

At the start of this chapter, I mentioned that direct internal dialogue is always written in first person and present tense. That makes it easy when you're writing in third person and past tense, but it can cause a bit of confusion around how to deal with direct dialogue in the other tenses and persons. Hang in there. I'll explain it all in Chapter Three: How to Format Internal Dialogue.

TAKE IT TO THE PAGE

Editing the internal dialogue in your manuscript doesn't come with as many shortcuts as some other writing craft elements do. Because of this, I'm providing you with two options for taking these concepts to the pages of your manuscript.

Option A is the quick-check version. In this version, you'll work on small passages or single chapters. The goal is to teach yourself the techniques while, at the same time, improving pieces of your work. The idea behind this option path is that, once you learn these techniques, you'll be better able to execute them while writing. When you do move to a full self-edit of your manuscript, you'll also be better able to spot problems areas and you'll know how to fix them.

Option B is the full revision version. In this version, you'll move through your manuscript multiple times or you'll wait on these exercises until you've read this book completely and you'll work through your full manuscript then.

Neither option path is better than the other. I give different options to suit different personality types and different time restrictions.

Option A – Quick-Check Version

Find a chapter where you have bad indirect internal dialogue. If you don't know where to start looking, use the Find feature in your word processing program to search for *wondered* or *realized*.

Is this section of internal dialogue pivotal to the plot?

If so, try rewriting it using a mixture of direct and indirect internal dialogue.

If not, try rewriting it using good indirect internal dialogue.

Not sure if you've succeeded? Try these tests:

1. Take your indirect internal dialogue and rewrite it in first person. Good indirect internal dialogue should sound smooth and natural when you change it from third person to first person. That's because internal dialogue is the character thinking to themselves.
2. Read the internal dialogue out loud. Could you imagine yourself saying these things? Does it read smoothly, or do you stumble over it?

Option B – Full Revision Version

Your option path will take longer. In each chapter, I'm giving you checks and revisions you can do, but I strongly recommend that you wait until you've finished reading this entire book. In Appendix E, I'll provide you with a single-pass, full-revision checklist so that you can do this as efficiently as possible.

If you want to do the exercises after reading each chapter, here's where to start.

As you make your first pass, highlight all passages of internal dialogue that you come across. Highlight the passages of bad indirect internal dialogue in a different color.

To save yourself headaches and paper, I recommend using the highlight feature in your word processing program. This way, when you fix a passage, you can also change its highlight color.

Keep all your internal dialogue passages highlighted. This will save you time later.

Here's what you should be asking yourself about each internal dialogue passage.

Question 1 – Is this passage bad indirect internal dialogue? If so, continue on to step 2. If not, move on to the next passage.

Question 2 – Is this section of internal dialogue really important? If so, try rewriting it using a mixture of direct and indirect internal dialogue. If not, try rewriting it using good indirect internal dialogue.

Not sure if you've succeeded? Try these tests:

1. Take your indirect internal dialogue and rewrite it in first person. Good indirect internal dialogue should sound smooth and natural when you change it from third person to first person. That's because internal dialogue is the character thinking to themselves.

2. Read the internal dialogue out loud. Could you imagine yourself saying these things? Does it read smoothly, or do you stumble over it?

If you'd like a printable version of the complete revision checklist (material from all the chapters) for your option track, go to **www.marcykennedy.com/internal-dialogue** and use the password **internaldialogue**.

CHAPTER THREE

How to Format Internal Dialogue

Now that you understand the difference between indirect and direct internal dialogue, we can talk about formatting. The question of "How do I format internal dialogue?" is actually three questions.

Should I use a tag like *she thought?*

Should I use italics?

Should I set internal dialogue off in its own paragraph?

The answers to those questions depend in part on whether you're using indirect internal dialogue or direct internal dialogue, which is why we had to look at those first. The answers also depend on what point of view (POV) you're writing in and what tense you want to use.

And the answers are a lot simpler than most people make it seem. In this chapter, I'm going to walk you through it from big picture to small scale, so we're going to talk about the unbreakable rules when it comes to formatting internal dialogue and then I'll explain the formatting differences between direct and indirect internal dialogue. From that point on, we'll break down how to format different types of direct internal dialogue based on point of view and tense.

We'll talk about whether or not to set internal dialogue off in its own paragraph in Chapter Five: How to Balance Internal Dialogue with External Action.

THE TWO RULES FOR FORMATTING INTERNAL DIALOGUE

As I mentioned earlier, when it comes to writing, I normally don't like to talk about "rules." So when I'm explaining how to format internal dialogue, I want you to think of these items as guidelines or best practices. Following these guidelines is the easiest, cleanest, least confusing way to handle it. Yes, you'll find books and writers who don't follow these guidelines. There are almost always exceptions to every craft item you'll be taught throughout your career. But these guidelines show you how you should normally act for the best results.

There are only two undisputed (and unbreakable) rules when it comes to formatting internal dialogue.

Rule #1 - Never use quotation marks for internal dialogue.

Quotation marks signal spoken dialogue. Placing your internal dialogue in quotation marks will confuse the reader.

Rule # 2 – Be consistent with whatever format you choose.

No matter how you choose to format your internal dialogue, the key is to be consistent. Readers are smart. As long as you're consistent (and don't use quotation marks), they'll be able to figure it out.

Additional Tip: While it's not a rule, you also normally shouldn't write something like *he thought to himself*. It's redundant. Who else would he be thinking to? Our thoughts are always to ourselves unless we're writing a story where the characters have telepathic abilities.

FORMATTING INDIRECT VS. DIRECT INTERNAL DIALOGUE

When you're trying to sort through how to format your internal dialogue, the first thing you need to decide is whether you're looking at indirect or direct internal dialogue.

Indirect internal dialogue shouldn't be given tags or set off in italics because you're not giving the reader the exact words of the character. In a sense, this makes it the easiest to deal with because you don't have to make a decision about italics or tags at all. I don't know of any writer who italicizes indirect internal dialogue.

Things become more complicated when we're working with direct internal dialogue. In direct internal dialogue, we can write it without tags or italics, with a tag but no italics, with a tag and italics, or with italics but no tag. What we choose depends on what point of view we're writing in.

TAGS AND ITALICS IN DIRECT INTERNAL DIALOGUE

In the examples below, I'm not trying to illustrate how the POVs themselves are different from each other. I'm trying to show you only how to format your internal dialogue. In other words, normally you'd also have differences in the content as well as the formatting based on the POV.

I've kept the wording as similar as possible (ignoring the way it would change based on POV changes) because I wanted to highlight the formatting. If I also illustrated the differences in how the POVs themselves would change the wording, it would make things more confusing.

(If you want to learn more about POV, please sign up for my newsletter at http://eepurl.com/Bk2Or to be notified when I release *Point of View in Fiction: A Busy Writer's Guide*.)

In Omniscient POV, Use Italics and a Tag

Omniscient POV is the point of view in which we're at the greatest risk of confusing the reader about who owns each thought. This situation arises because omniscient POV maintains distance from each character, the narrator has access to every character's mind, and the author's voice is dominant.

In stories written in omniscient POV, readers are also at risk of confusion over whether the thoughts they're hearing belong to a character at all or whether they belong to the omniscient narrator. In omniscient POV, it's important that the reader be able to differentiate between the thoughts and opinions of the characters and the thoughts and opinions of the narrator/author.

For this reason, I recommend using a tag along with italics in most situations.

> Ronald took Melody's hand and flashed her a smile fit for a dentist's ad. "I'll pay you back."
> *Liar*, she thought. *Where's the $1000 you still owe me?* "I'm maxed out this month."

The reason we want to use tags sparingly in the other POVs is that tags add distance. Tags make the thoughts feel more reported and told rather than feeling experienced (as if the reader were inside the character, overhearing them).

That's not a big problem in omniscient POV because omniscient POV has a more distant feel from the characters to begin with. The reader knows that someone (the narrator/author) is telling them the story.

For more on how to properly format tags in internal dialogue, please read Appendix D: How to Use Tags in Internal Dialogue. They're handled almost identically to tags attached to spoken dialogue.

In Limited Third-Person POV, Use Only Italics

Limited third-person POV stories can be written in either past tense or present tense, and your internal dialogue can look a little different depending on which tense you choose. Let's look at past tense first because it's the most straightforward.

> Ronald took Melody's hand and flashed her a smile fit for a dentist's ad. "I'll pay you back."
> Melody yanked her hand away. *Liar. Where's the $1000 you still owe me?* "I'm maxed out this month."

Because we're in limited third-person point of view, we'll already know that any thoughts are Melody's, so we don't need the "she thought" of omniscient POV. The italics clue the reader in that we're now hearing Melody's exact thoughts.

You don't have to add the action beat in front of the internal dialogue to make it work, but I wanted to show you that it sometimes helps to ground the reader.

While you could technically write your direct internal dialogue in third person with a tag and no italics or with no tag and no italics, I strongly recommend against it. Remember that direct internal dialogue is written in first-person present tense. If your story is in third-person past tense and you drop in a few lines of first-person present tense, it jars the reader.

Take a look:

> Ronald took Melody's hand and flashed her a smile fit for a dentist's ad. "I'll pay you back."
> Melody yanked her hand away. Liar. Where's the $1000 you still owe me? "I'm maxed out this month."

It feels like something is wrong and can be confusing. We don't want our writing to feel clunky to our readers. It breaks their engagement with the story. We need to always be thinking about the best interests of our readers. Anything that makes them pause, hesitate, or stumble is bad.

Now what changes if we're writing in third-person present tense?

Because our story is still in third person but our direct internal dialogue is in first person, we format it exactly the same.

> Ronald takes Melody's hand and flashes her a smile fit for a dentist's ad. "I'll pay you back."
> Melody yanks her hand away. *Liar. Where's the $1000 you still owe me?* "I'm maxed out this month."

Additional Tip: How to choose the tense of your story is a topic that's outside the scope of this book. Past tense is the most common, but successful books—for example, *The Help* and *The Hunger Games*—have been written in present tense. That said, writing in present tense is challenging to do well. If you're considering present tense, do your research, try a few chapters both ways, and make sure your choice is the best one strategically for your particular story. Then be ready to put in the extra work necessary to make a present tense story flow.

For First Person, Consider Your Tense

Internal dialogue in first-person POV causes the most problems for writers. We're deep inside our character's head, the character is the one narrating the story directly, and our reader will understand that what they're reading is exactly what the character is thinking. The line between narration and internal dialogue is extremely unstable and blurry in first person POV.

That doesn't mean, though, that formatting direct internal dialogue in first person needs to be confusing.

When we're writing in first-person past tense and our internal dialogue is in past tense, we don't need italics or any other signal. The trick with this is that we must maintain a consistent tense. We can't switch to present tense in our internal dialogue if we're otherwise writing in past tense.

> Ronald took my hand and flashed me a smile fit for a dentist's ad. "I'll pay you back."
> Liar. Where was the $1000 he still owed me? "I'm maxed out this month."

If we're writing in past tense and we want to put our direct internal dialogue in present tense, then we need to set it off with italics so the tense switch doesn't unbalance our reader. If we want, we can also use a tag. In first person, tags don't create the same sense of distance that they can when we're writing in omniscient or limited third-person POV.

> Ronald took my hand and flashed me a smile fit for a dentist's ad. "I'll pay you back."
> *Liar*, I thought. *Where's the $1000 you still owe me?* "I'm maxed out this month."

You can see how Neil Gaiman uses this technique in his first-person POV book *The Ocean at the End of the Lane.* The narrator is telling the story in past tense, but when he writes his exact thoughts, he switches into present tense the same way spoken dialogue is in present tense. To avoid confusion, Gaiman sets these off with both italics and tags.

WHAT DO I DO IF I'M WRITING A PARANORMAL, FANTASY, OR SCIENCE FICTION STORY AND PEOPLE CAN SPEAK TELEPATHICALLY?

This is actually the trickiest of all because now you're juggling externally spoken dialogue, internal dialogue where the character is thinking to herself, and head speak where two characters are speaking privately in their minds.

Here's what I recommend to keep it all straight.

Use quotation marks for normal dialogue spoken out loud.

For internal dialogue where your characters are thinking to themselves, stick to indirect internal dialogue.

That way, you don't need either italics or tags and you can save them for the head speak.

For head speak, use italics.

The first time this happens, you'll need to use a tag or signal to the reader somehow that they're talking in their heads. Once you establish that italics mean "we're talking telepathically," the reader will assume that's the case every time they see italics. This is why you can't then also use italics for internal dialogue where the character is thinking to herself.

So for the sake of demonstration, let's assume Ronald and Melody from our earlier example are telepaths now, and they've met up with a third character named Edgar, who owns a classic space cruiser that Ronald desperately wants to buy.

> "Sorry, bro." Edgar rolled his three eyes. "I need cash now, not someday after you've been flying her for months."
>
> Ronald took my hand. *Loan me the money?* he asked telepathically. *I'll pay you back.*
>
> Liar. Where was the $1000 he still owed me? I yanked my hand away. *I'm maxed out this month. You'll have to ask your sister.*

If you use this technique consistently, your readers will easily understand what's happening.

TAKE IT TO THE PAGE

Option A – Quick-Check Version

For this option path, the key is to look at enough chapters to see if you've gotten this right or not.

If you haven't, make yourself a note for when you're revising and make sure you apply consistent formatting then.

Microsoft Word provides a great quick trick if you notice you've italicized internal dialogue that you shouldn't have. Go to Find, and then choose Advanced Find. A box will pop up. Make sure your cursor is blinking in the "Find what:" box. Now, select Format and then Font. Select Italics and click OK.

When you hit Find Next, Word will take you instance by instance through all your italicized items.

Option B – Full Revision Version

In the last chapter, you highlighted all your internal dialogue. This makes it easy for you to skim through and fix any formatting problems.

Make a mental note of the mistakes you normally make so you can get it right in your first draft next time.

CHAPTER FOUR

How to Use Internal Dialogue to Advance the Story

What we as writers call *internal dialogue*, psychologists call *self-talk*.

Self-talk is part of how we evaluate and form opinions on everything that happens to us, good or bad, and it influences how we feel and behave.

Self-talk comes in two forms—constructive and destructive.

Destructive self-talk is when you criticize yourself, call yourself names, second-guess yourself, or project the worst into the future. *Constructive self-talk* does the opposite. You build yourself up, think optimistically about the future, and actively problem-solve.

Self-talk for most people happens nearly non-stop throughout their day, even when writing up a grocery list, driving to a new location, or figuring out what project to work on next at their job. For our characters, though, we can't show absolutely every thought that passes through their heads. We shouldn't.

In Chapter One, I gave you one of the few inviolable rules when it comes to internal dialogue—only share thoughts that advance the story.

That rule raises the question of what type of internal dialogue counts as advancing the story. What should we share and what shouldn't we? How can we best use internal dialogue in our stories?

And that's what this chapter is about.

I'm going to walk you through the effective uses of internal dialogue, starting with characterization, moving on to plot progression, and finishing with the more subtle elements like enhancing theme and setting the mood.

Please remember that there can be quite a bit of overlap between the uses. So, for example, just because a piece of internal dialogue reveals character doesn't mean it can't also move the plot forward. In fact, the best internal dialogue serves more than one purpose simultaneously.

With that in mind, here we go.

REVEAL YOUR CHARACTER'S PERSONALITY

Internal dialogue advances the story when it shows the reader some important element of the point-of-view character.

We're our most honest in our self-talk because no one else is listening. This is also true when it comes to your character's internal dialogue. And because it's when they're at their most honest, their most uninhibited, it can also reveal a lot about them.

I'll give you an example from a sweet romance I'm working on.

She handed him the manila folder. "Everything is there from my previous doctors. My audiogram, the results of my auditory brainstem response test, and the CD with my MRI pictures." She drew a deep breath. There, that was another coherent sentence. Maybe she was going to be able to manage this. He was a medical professional after all, not a prospective date.

"Previous doctors? You've had more than one?"

"You're the fifth."

He cocked an eyebrow at her. "I see." His long fingers flipped through the pages in her file. "Acoustic neuroma. You're a bit young for that."

Gratefulness flooded through her that he'd said *acoustic neuroma* rather than the more blunt *tumor*. *Acoustic neuroma* sounded scientific. An acoustic neuroma she could research and beat. A tumor brought back memories of her grandmother's last days.

From the internal dialogue alone, we learn a lot about this character. She's much less confident on the inside than she appears on the outside. She feels more in control when things stay clinical and scientific rather than delving into the realm of emotions.

How, specifically, is this done, though? It's one thing to say we should use internal dialogue to reveal our character's personality, and another thing to break it down into practical, actionable ways to do this.

Before we move on to how internal dialogue can move our plot forward, I'll give you six ways we can use internal dialogue to help reveal our character's personality: showing emotional vulnerability, differentiating between characters, interpreting and passing judgment on events and setting, showing character growth, hinting at backstory, and adding touches of humor.

Show Emotional Vulnerability

You could consider this an offshoot of revealing a character's personality traits. In this case, however, we're not revealing their traits. We're revealing their weaknesses, fears, and insecurities. We're showing them empathize with the pain of others, even if they can't do anything about that pain. Using internal dialogue in this way is like flipping your character over and exposing their soft underbelly to the reader. Our characters should never be like the rock monster in *Galaxy Quest* that had no vulnerable spots.

While using internal dialogue to reveal your characters' vulnerabilities makes any character more relatable and likeable, it's especially important if you've created a character who is outwardly confident, perfect, hard-shelled, or abrasive. Internal dialogue can help readers bond with an otherwise hard-to-like character.

Let's look at the positive side first—a very confident, self-assured character or a character who is good at almost everything they do. A too-perfect character can be hard to relate to and might seem unrealistic. No one I know of is perfect, and the people who seem to have it all together on the surface are usually just putting on a show. We don't tend to like those people in real life (in part because we're a bit jealous of them).

Readers can also have a difficult time connecting with these too-good-to-be-true characters because they can seem to lack depth. They come across as flat. That lack of dimension or layers makes them uninteresting.

One way to solve either of those issues is to show, through internal dialogue, that the character isn't nearly as self-assured or perfect inside as the face they put on for the world makes it seem.

On the other side is a hard-shelled or abrasive character. These types of characters need to be humanized by showing that they might not like the way they are, or they have a soft spot for someone else, or they're frightened. We can foster reader connection with them by using internal dialogue to reveal their vulnerable parts.

One of the main characters in my co-written historical fantasy *The Amazon Heir* (not yet released) is a fierce woman warrior, an Amazon. Because of the restrictions of her society and the role she needs to play in it, she has to show a hard exterior to the world. Any sign of weakness or mercy could result in her death.

Here's a selection from one of our first drafts. In this scene, Zerynthia, our Amazon, is participating in a bull-leaping competition. Before her turn comes to jump, she watches the other competitors. The bull-leaping is an essential tradition in their society, where only the strongest and best have a chance to win. (The Greens are the farmer class within Amazonian society.)

> The girl leaped. The bull lifted his horns and caught the inside of her leg, opening her from knee to groin. She bounced off his hindquarters and hit the ground. Her screams rent the air.
>
> Three Greens rushed to her side. One pressed both hands on the open gash to staunch the gushing fountain erupting from the girl's inner thigh. The girl writhed.
>
> Zerynthia stayed where she was. Even the strongest warrior did not survive such a wound, and she was young. No number of hands would spare her.
>
> Reds hauled the bull away by the tethers. The Greens carried the lifeless girl out, her body limp in their arms.

Early feedback from beta readers and critique groups told us that readers found Zerynthia cold and unlikeable. This moment was one in particular that they pointed out. Zerynthia shows no mercy for the dying girl, externally or internally. That wasn't what we intended. We couldn't change her external actions without compromising her character and making her inauthentic to her culture and time.

But we could show more of her true character through her internal dialogue.

> Three Greens rushed to her side. One pressed both hands on the open gash to staunch the gushing fountain erupting from the girl's inner thigh. The girl writhed.
>
> Zerynthia's stomach writhed along with her. She took a step forward and stopped herself. She must stay where she was, for appearance's sake. Even the strongest warrior did not survive such a wound. No number of hands would spare her, and to comfort the dying girl would be seen as weakness. The dead had no value to Amazonia, deprived of even a name in memory. It would not remain so once she became queen.

Internal dialogue allows us to show readers our character's true self and what they want to do even if they're not able to do it.

Differentiate Between Characters

All writers face the challenge of making their characters unique individuals rather than cardboard cutouts or replicas of the author. It's not easy. Sometimes our characters are clear and unique in our minds, but it doesn't transfer to the page.

Internal dialogue is one way we can differentiate between our characters. We can take two (or more) of our point-of-view characters and show their different opinions on and approaches to the same situation. In giving their differing perspectives on the same event, news, or person, we start to show the reader what the characters are like and how they're different.

If your characters face a challenge together, the internal dialogue you give to each POV character can show one of them approaching it with optimism, while the other is more doubtful about their chances of success. One can approach a setback with humor, while the other approaches it as a puzzle to solve.

As another example, we might have a situation in our story where one character needs to take a risk that puts her life in danger. Through her internal dialogue, we can show that she feels this risk is calculated and that there's no other way to achieve what needs to be achieved. When we switch POV, we can show a different character who interprets the same actions as reckless.

Whatever the situation, the principle behind this is to show how each character interprets the situation slightly differently.

In my historical fantasy *Cursed Wishes* (releasing early 2016), my female main character, Ceana, believes you should grab at opportunities when they arise. My male main character, Gavran, is the opposite. He wants to plan things out. Because of how I weave their personalities in through their interpretation of events, I never have to tell the reader that Ceana is the decisive, seize-the-moment one and Gavran is the careful contingency planner. Their internal dialogue shows their personalities and helps differentiate them.

I'll give you two passages as examples with the key lines of internal dialogue bolded and underlined.

Passage 1: Ceana's Point of View

The sky was already lighter than when he'd first woken her. The men could rise any moment. She followed Gavran back through the trees. Maybe she should ask him what changed his mind. **But opportunities didn't linger for the hesitant. They favored those who chased them.**

Passage 2: Gavran's Point of View

As soon as they were out of the tent, she reached for his pocket. "Let me see it."

He brushed her hands away. "You heard what she said. Not here."

"I won't drink it. I just want to hold it."

He wouldn't let her impulsiveness win this time.

Look where that'd gotten them last night.

This also works for setting descriptions. When we add internal dialogue to a description of setting, it brings the setting to life and makes it interesting rather than something people will skim. Every time we describe setting, we should filter it through the current opinion and mood of the point-of-view character.

For example, let's say we have two sisters returning to the home they grew up in after their mother has passed away.

Sister #1's Point of View:

Miranda stopped less than a foot inside the front door. The heavy blackout drapes smothered any light that tried to enter through the windows, but the sunshine behind her cast shadows from their mother's hard-backed chair. At least there'd be no lectures today. And if Evelyn didn't want to save every worthless trinket, they could be done by dark and list the house for sale tomorrow.

Sister #2's Point of View:

Evelyn walked to the middle of the living room and rested a hand on the back of the plush couch that always seemed to welcome her when she came for advice. Their mother's reading glasses still nestled on the hand-carved end table their grandfather gave her parents as a wedding gift. Tears clogged her throat. What was she going to do now without either of them to go to for guidance when she needed it?

Because we've seen how each sister judges the setting, I don't have to tell you how they each individually felt about their mother. It's there, coloring their perception of the world around them.

Even description should never be just description. It should always serve a greater purpose in the story.

The technique of using internal dialogue to differentiate between characters only works if you have multiple point-of-view characters. The remaining techniques work regardless of how many point-of-view characters you have.

Interpret and Pass Judgment

One of the qualities that make a deep point of view (also known as close or intimate point of view) so engaging for readers is seeing through the eyes of another person—listening to them interpret the world around them and pass judgment on it through their internal dialogue. Allow your characters to have an opinion and attitude about what's happening to them and around them.

I'll give you an example. This is from Randy Ingermanson and John Olson's *Oxygen*. The point-of-view character, Bob, is a mechanical engineer-turned-astronaut who is part of the crew for the first manned mission to Mars. In this scene, Bob is running on a treadmill and the NASA director comes in with a woman. Bob overhears that her name is Valkerie. The director is called away, leaving Valkerie to look around unattended.

> Bob suppressed a grin as the reporter immediately walked over to inspect the waste-recycling bioreactor. The last reporter to escape her leash had managed to contaminate an air-recycling rig that had been in continuous operation for over a year. Heads were still rolling after that one. If looks were any indicator, this one might be capable of taking out an entire building.

Based on Valkerie's name and appearance, Bob's interpretation of the situation is that Valkerie is a reporter who will bungle up anything she touches. He passes judgment based on what he sees, and we also receive his opinion of reporters—they're troublesome and not very smart, but they're good for a laugh. It also hints that he might be wary of beautiful women.

Bob, however, is completely wrong. Valkerie is a medical doctor brought in as the final member of the Mars mission team.

That's one of the great ways we're able to use internal dialogue. We can use a character's first impressions of a situation and play with that. Are they right? Are they wrong? What misunderstandings and conflict will grow out of their interpretation?

Show Character Growth

Character growth, also known as a character arc, is the beating heart of every story. Renowned writing instructor and author David Farland wrote about character creation that "Stories aren't about characters so much as they are about growth. In other words, your characters will change and grow throughout a novel, and it isn't necessarily the character herself that is interesting, but that process of change."[1]

Many things go into creating a character that readers will want to follow through the course of an entire story, but change is one of the secret keys to keeping a reader engaged. Change and growth are inherently interesting to us as human beings.

Internal dialogue isn't the only tool we'll need to build a character arc, but it is a requirement for a believable one. Internal dialogue helps show how a character's thoughts and beliefs change over the course of the story.

Let's look at an example.

---

[1] http://www.davidfarland.com/writing_tips/?a=213

In Jami Gold's paranormal romance novel *Treasured Claim*, the main character is Elaina Drake. She's a dragon who hasn't yet accumulated enough treasure to ignite her heart and be able to shapeshift from human to dragon form.

Elaina's growth arc deals with the fact that she has always believed dragons are incapable of love. She's currently hiding from her father because he killed her mother and now wants to kill her.

I'm going to give you a few examples taken from different points in *Treasured Claim* to show you how Gold uses internal dialogue to help build Elaina's character growth.

The first sample comes from early on, in Chapter Eight, shortly after Elaina has met and had her first kiss with Alex, the hero of the story.

> At her kitchen table, she flipped Alex's money clip over in her palm. Her thumb caressed the dragon shape on its surface, and her forehead thumped onto the tabletop.
>
> She really was an idiot. A huge, almost overpowering, part of her wanted to return to him.
>
> And then what? Even in the best-case scenario, without the threat from her father, they'd have a hard time making things work between them. They'd argue about her taking jewelry. Or worse, she'd capitulate to his human laws and stay weak forever, unable to ignite her heart and change form, constantly on the verge of death.
>
> No, it was better this way. Love wasn't possible for dragons, and it didn't conquer all anyway. Her mother had paid the price for that fallacy.

As the story progresses, we start to see through her internal dialogue that Elaina wishes things could be different (the first step to change). For example...

Too bad dragons couldn't love, because for once, she wished it could be possible.

And the longer she spends with Alex, the more she mentally adjusts her idea of what love is. Her experience has been so narrow that her view of love is warped, and part of how she grows over the course of the story is in her understanding of what *love* really means—the second step to lasting change is destroying false preconceptions. To show Elaina changing, Gold weaves in little snippets like this:

Love was more complicated and nuanced than she'd guessed.

Near the end of the book, with help from an old friend, Elaina finally accepts that love *is* possible for dragons. Gold marks this culmination of Elaina's character arc with internal dialogue.

She climbed onto the mound of coins and draped her arms around his neck, speaking to him in Drakish once more. "I am proud to call you Great Father."
He rested his chin along her back. The sense of love and security coming off his body enveloped her like a blanket. There was no doubt that dragons *could* love.

I used this example in part because I wanted to point out something important. Even though there are other passages throughout the book, Gold never has Elaina think about whether or not dragons can love for more than a paragraph or two at a time. Internal dialogue should be used as one method to show character growth, but it shouldn't be done in a heavy-handed way. It needs to arise organically from story events, and it needs to be complemented by external action. The two work together in tandem.

Hint at Backstory

One of the common writing "sins" we can easily fall in to is backstory dump. A backstory dump happens when we stop the present-day story to tell the reader what happened prior to the start of the book. The way to avoid backstory dump is to hint at backstory or to weave it in using nibbles. We can use spoken dialogue for this, but we can also use internal dialogue.

Internal dialogue is an excellent way to do this because we do naturally think back on our past when something in the present triggers a memory. (However, we're not likely to stand around for five minutes reminiscing to ourselves. It'll be a quick thought.)

We can use these hints of backstory to help develop motivation for our character's present-day actions. (Remember, at the start of the chapter, I mentioned many of these ways to use internal dialogue to move the story forward would overlap each other.)

Mystery author Kassandra Lamb does an excellent job is this in her thriller *Fatal Forty-Eight*. Skip Canfield is a private investigator and one of the main characters in *Fatal Forty-Eight*. His wife's former colleague has been kidnapped by a serial killer, and Skip's investigation agency is working with the local police and the FBI to find her. Skip has very little patience for people who are rude or haughty, and that's exactly how Special Agent Julie Wallace seems when Skip meets her. As the story goes on, however, his perspective on her starts to change.

> Skip spotted Judith Anderson and SA Wallace a block away. He waved but they didn't see him. He started jogging in their direction.
>
> Wallace tugged her suit jacket across her chest.
>
> Skip sucked in his breath. He recognized the gesture. She wasn't cold. She was trying to hide her assets.

When a late growth spurt had turned the scrawny teenager he had once been into a hunk, he'd quickly learned that attractiveness was both a blessing and a curse. No doubt Wallace's voluptuous figure made her life tough at the FBI.

Lamb used internal dialogue to slide in a bit of information about Skip's past. It feels natural because Skip has a reason to be thinking about his own past here. There's an external cue that triggers his memory.

This snippet of backstory in the internal dialogue becomes an important part of Skip's motivation for being extra kind to SA Wallace. He starts to recognize that, despite her external coldness and superiority, she's actually very insecure. Because of how Lamb had developed Skip's character in earlier books in the series, she needed to show *why* Skip would take SA Wallace under his wing, especially since his unusual treatment of her ends up making his wife jealous.

We can also use internal dialogue to give enough of a hint at the backstory of a character that it piques the reader's interest and makes them want to keep turning pages. As an editor, I often work with authors who are confused about how much and what to withhold from readers. Backstory is something we should withhold and deal out in small pieces, giving the reader just enough so they're not confused and only sharing it when it becomes pertinent to the present-day story.

I'll give you an example before we move on. This is another example from my historical fantasy *Cursed Wishes*. Part of the important backstory in this novel is Ceana Campbell's relationship with her brother. Just before the section I'll show you below, Ceana has learned that the family who nursed her back to health has burned her clothes because they were full of lice and too worn to save.

Ceana's fingernails cut into her palms even through the fabric of the blanket. Davina seemed to float further away, and roaring filled Ceana's ears. If her clothes were gone, so were the ribbons her dadaidh gave her when her brother was born. They were the one thing of value she'd managed to protect. Her last piece of her family. Her last tie to one of her few happy memories of her family before what she'd done to her brother turned her dadaidh to drink and made him hate her.

I used this example because I wanted to point out another important element of weaving backstory in through internal dialogue. Even though we want to withhold some information from the reader, we still need to give them enough specifics that they're interested.

From the passage above, it's clear that the reason Ceana's father hates her has something to do with an incident between her and her brother. It wouldn't have been enough to say "what she'd done." That could mean anything. By adding in a little more, without giving too much away, we can walk that fine line between providing the reader with so much that they're not curious anymore and providing them with so little that they're confused (and therefore uninterested).

Adding Touches of Humor

Allow me to start this section with a caveat. Not every character needs to be funny and not every story needs humor in it to work. Whether or not we employ humor depends on our personal writing voice and on our intended audience. So filter all the remaining recommendations in this section through that lens. Humor is a nice additive in the right situation. It's not a requirement.

Humor in internal dialogue immediately sets a character apart because not everyone has a sense of humor. By choosing to use humor in one character's internal dialogue and choosing not to use it in another's, we're already distinguishing between them.

We can take this a step deeper, though. What type of sense of humor do they have? Dry? Snarky? Corny? Crass?

It matters because it says something about them as a person, and you can convey that to the reader through their humor.

I'll give you an example from Ingermanson and Olson's *Oxygen* again.

> His shower had already expired. If he didn't find her soon, the date police were going to permanently revoke his right to bear armpits.

This internal dialogue comes from Bob, one of the main characters. His POV scenes are full of lines like this. If I shared a few more, even out of context, you would start to get the idea that Bob is intelligent, a bit of a geek, and doesn't have a high opinion of himself in social situations. All of that comes out just through his corny, self-deprecating sense of humor.

This is also where you need to consider your audience. For example, if you know that your audience is older church-going women, they'll view a character who uses crass humor differently than will most twenty-something male readers.

The quote from *Oxygen* above is another good example. One of the things that appealed to me about the novel was Bob's sense of humor, but not everyone would find it as funny as I did. I liked Bob more as a character because his sense of humor matched mine.

The flip side of this is to show, through internal dialogue, what your characters find funny, even if they don't have the capability to be funny themselves. What makes us laugh speaks volumes about us.

I'll give you an example. My dad loves shows like *Funniest Home Videos* where people are always crashing into things. Slapstick humor makes him laugh. I don't enjoy those types of shows at all. All I can see are the things that could have gone terribly wrong—that fall that was funny because everyone walked away with minor bruises could just as easily have been a broken neck. Our personalities—my tendency to worry and my dad's tendency to take life as it comes—are reflected in our humor preferences.

MOVES THE PLOT FORWARD

If I were to ask what the most important element of fiction is, I'd guess that very few people would say internal dialogue. But internal dialogue forms part of the engine for moving your plot forward. It helps readers understand what's happening and why. It raises tension and conflict. A story needs it to function.

Slide in Information Your Reader Needs to Know

Using internal dialogue to slide in information your reader needs to know can cause problems. If not executed correctly, it can lead to an as-I-know version of the As-You-Know-Bob Syndrome found in spoken dialogue.

As the name suggests, As-You-Know-Bob Syndrome is when one character tells another character something they already know. It's done purely for the reader's benefit, and it's unnatural. This becomes even more unnatural when you have a character thinking about something they wouldn't normally think about or when you have them think about it in a way they wouldn't.

To avoid this, make sure your point-of-view character has a reason to be thinking about that bit of information now.

I'll show you an example of how Ingermanson and Olson used internal dialogue to handle one of the most dreaded problems we face—how to naturally describe our point-of-view character. In this passage, Bob struggles to put on an Extra-Vehicular Activity suit (an

EVA). Throughout the whole scene, Ingermanson and Olson sneak in information about this suit that the reader will need to know later. You see Josh, the astronaut in charge of the mission, easily donning the suit, and Bob failing miserably. Josh tries to help Bob, but eventually has to stop to finish with his own suit. Bob has stepped into the pants, but still has to get the top half of the suit on. It's hanging from the wall, and Josh suggests that Bob squat down and slide up into it from underneath.

> *I'm on my own now.* Bob let go of the circular metal ring that ran around the belt of the pants. He squatted and tried to back in underneath the suit. Which was practically impossible for a guy almost six feet tall. Josh had it easy—he was five inches shorter and a lot more limber.

We get a touch of description about the appearance of these men. Bob wouldn't normally think about their height difference, but in this situation, it's natural.

Build Internal Conflict

One of the strengths of internal dialogue in fiction is how it shows the reader indecision in the character—those moments when they don't know what to do or they don't know what decision is the right one to make. It also allows us to show a character justifying what might otherwise be considered an obviously wrong decision. These decisions by our point-of-view character, the way they work through this inner conflict to pick their next step, is part of what drives the direction our story will take.

Here's an example:

> Duncan leaned close to the Malevich painting as if trying to parse meaning from the geometric and abstract shapes on the canvas. He squinted. Million-dollar piece of art and the gallery hadn't even encased it in glass. Pressure

sensitive alarm maybe? He should've asked for more money to do this job. The ones that looked the easiest always came back to bite him.

An arm linked through his. He tamped down the natural guilt responses of jumping or stiffening, prepared his response about doubting the authenticity of the signature, and turned to face the guard.

The person belonging to the hand wasn't the guard he expected. A woman with a runner's body and golden brown eyes that would have made even him give up a life of crime—almost—smiled up at him.

"I'm so sorry to do this to you." She whispered the words in the same tone one would speak to a lover. "But my ex-boyfriend is two paintings over with the woman he cheated on me with. I needed to look like I wasn't here alone."

It could be a trick. She could be undercover security hired by the gallery. Or she could be telling the truth.

She glanced over her shoulder in the direction of the supposed ex. A hard swallow shuddered down her throat, and he felt it like a jab to his kidney.

Duncan has no way of knowing if this is a trap or not. Hearing his internal dialogue allows us to see the conflict building inside him—does he trust this woman's story or doesn't he? Should he help her or shouldn't he? He wants to help her, but he realizes she might be playing him, trying to earn his sympathy so he'll let down his guard. In his business, that could cost him. Plus, he has a job to do and she's a distraction, along with being a potential threat.

Depending on whether the reader thinks she's playing him for a fool or not, they'll be rooting for him to come to one decision or the other. And that's part of the beauty of using internal dialogue to build inner conflict. Not only does the reader see what's going on behind the curtain, but they also become involved. They enjoy comparing how they would think and feel in that situation to how the character thinks and feels.

Develop Motivation

Motivation is the *why* behind your characters' actions. If you leave it out, it's like watching TV without the sound. Everyone is moving around and doing things, but you can't get a sense of what's really happening or the importance of it. Motivation is what makes our character's actions make sense.

Motivation is important on two levels in fiction—the big-picture story level and the small-scale paragraph-by-paragraph level or scene-by-scene level. Internal dialogue can help us develop motivation at both levels.

In terms of the big-picture story level, motivation and goals are often confused.

A goal is something concrete. The motivation is why the character wants that goal.

In my short story "The Replacements," in my ebook *Frozen*, my main character is an antihero. She ran away from home, and now wants to return. As she pulls up to her parents' house, she finds children playing on her parents' lawn. As the story progresses, she's going to kidnap those children, believing that she won't be welcomed home as long as they're there. It's a horrible action, and so she needed a strong motivation for stealing the children away. She also needed a strong motivation for why she had to act quickly, rather than waiting to figure out a different solution.

And all of that had to be done without using spoken dialogue because she had to feel completely isolated and alone. She's smart enough to realize she'd be stopped if anyone knew what she planned to do. For these reasons, I had to use internal dialogue to establish her motivation.

"One more time around. Slowly."

He grunted. "It's your money."

The cab eased away from the curb. She squinted through the dusty back window. She didn't have money to waste. Enough for the cab bill and a hotel room maybe. She'd assumed she'd come home and they'd kill the fatted calf. She hadn't figured on paying for anything other than the bus ticket and cab ride here. They should have spotted her in the cab, flung open the door, embraced her. Should've, could've, would've.

The children shrunk until their golden heads painted two splotches on the green grass like two dandelions. They were the dandelions; she was the firstborn. If they weren't there, her parents would give her the welcome she'd imagined every day for the last six months while she sat through rehab and counseling. She wasn't going back to the shelter. Or the streets. Or Eddie. She wanted to go home, and she could if she weeded out the dandelions in her lawn.

Let me give you another example of how you can use internal dialogue to establish a big decision the main character is going to make, a decision that will influence the course of the plot.

In Lindsay Buroker's *Encrypted*, her main character Tikaya Komitopis helped her country as a cryptologist during the war, decoding enemy communications. The Turgonians (the enemy nation) blame her for the fact that they lost the war with her country. She's been warned by her president that, if they figure out her identity, they'll try to kill her.

Early on in the book, the Turgonians find Tikaya and want to kidnap her from her home. All other things being equal, you'd expect Tikaya to do whatever it takes to hide so they can't find her. Buroker needs to establish a strong motivation for Tikaya to do the opposite—to go with them and help the enemy. Here's how Buroker does it:

> If men waited outside, Tikaya could not see them, but that meant little. Perhaps they were crouched beside the doors, ready to pounce. Maybe they were already in the house, threatening her family. Or worse. If anything happened to her kin, it was her fault. She swallowed. She had to make sure the soldiers focused on her.

Prior to this point, Buroker had established, also through internal dialogue, how important Tikaya's family is to her. She loves them. And when faced with the choice of sacrificing herself or putting her family in danger, Tikaya chooses to sacrifice herself.

Buroker used internal dialogue to give a strong motivation for why Tikaya would do something that would otherwise seem foolhardy.

Both of these examples illustrate why it's so important to use internal dialogue to establish motivation. Everything our characters do needs to be consistent with their personalities and believable to the reader. Internal dialogue allows the reader to look inside the character's brain and understand why they do what they do.

Using internal dialogue to develop motivation works on a small scene-by-scene basis as well. Our main characters need a strong motivation for pursuing their large story goal, but they also need strong motivation for each action they take throughout the course of the story.

I once edited a story where the main character suddenly chopped off his hand. The character's goal was to evade the authorities who were hunting him, but the writer didn't first establish a reason (motivation) for chopping off his hand. My instinctive reaction was "That was stupid of him. Why did he do that?" I could see all the reasons this act would impede his goal, and I wasn't given any reasons why it would help his goal. Not only was I confused, but I disliked the character because he seemed foolish and reckless.

We never want a reader to feel like our character is stupid or to not understand why they're acting the way they are. When that happens, the reader ends up confused (which leads to them putting the book down).

React to Setbacks and Establish New Goals

If you've read Dwight Swain's *Techniques of the Selling Writer* or Randy Ingermanson's *Writing Fiction for Dummies*, then you'll be familiar with the concept of scenes and sequels (or what Ingermanson calls action scenes and reaction scenes).

In an action scene, the character has a goal, faces obstacles, and (usually) fails to achieve the scene goal. In a reaction scene, the character deals with the emotional fallout of their failure, considers their options, and sets a new goal.

Internal dialogue becomes a valuable tool in reaction scenes. We can use it to show our character's reaction to setbacks and we can also use it to show them working through their new options and choosing one. The more momentous the decision our character needs to make, the more internal dialogue we need to spend on the decision.

Remember, though, that internal dialogue isn't the only element we should use in reaction scenes. We should balance it with dialogue, visceral reactions, and external action. We'll look at achieving this balance more in a later chapter.

USING INTERNAL DIALOGUE IN THE SUBTLER ELEMENTS

The majority of this chapter has been devoted to the ways internal dialogue develops our characters and their arc or moves the physical, external plot forward. Internal dialogue can also be used to enhance the less straightforward elements of our fiction.

Develop the Theme

Earlier on, I gave the example of how Jami Gold used internal dialogue to develop her main character's arc in *Treasured Claim*. Even though we looked at that example through the lens of the character arc, our story's theme is, in essence, the lesson our main character learns over the course of the story. It's the message we want the reader to walk away from our story with.

If we're too obvious with the theme, the reader can feel preached to. One of the best ways to avoid this is to have different point-of-view characters struggle with the theme or message, each revealing a side of the issue or an opinion that differs from the others.

By now, I hope you can see how developing the theme is tightly tied together with not only developing the main character's arc, but also with other uses for internal dialogue, such as differentiating between characters.

Enhance the Mood

Rather than being something distinct we do with internal dialogue, enhancing the theme or mood has to do with the tone of the internal dialogue we use. Imagine a situation where your main character is walking home alone down a dark street.

If you wanted to set a humorous tone, you might have her noticing the smell of urine or some other yucky details of the world around her.

If you wanted to set a dark tone, you might have her thinking about the isolation of the situation she's in and how she used to sleep with a flashlight as a child.

If you wanted to set a hopeful tone, you could have her noticing how bright the stars are without streetlights blocking them out.

What our characters choose to think about, and the word choices they use to describe something, can set the mood for the scene.

Add Subtext

Subtext is what's happening underneath the words we've written. It's an unspoken message.

Subtext should weave throughout our stories, but one area where it works particularly well is in dialogue when two (or more) characters can't speak openly for some reason. It might be that they're afraid of being overheard, it might be that one of them doesn't feel safe expressing their true feelings, or it might be that one of them doesn't want to implicate themselves by saying anything directly.

For example, say we have a wife who is arguing with her husband about how he never replaces the empty toilet paper roll. You can show through her internal dialogue that this really has nothing to do with the toilet paper roll. It has everything to do with the fact that he leaves all the housework up to her even though she's working as many hours as he is. But she doesn't feel safe having that conversation. She's afraid of how he'll react if she shares her true feelings.

Or we might have our main character talking to the woman whose job our character won. The woman wants to make a threat, but she doesn't want to implicate herself by saying anything openly, so instead she talks about the plant she killed. Internal dialogue allows us to show that our main character understands this woman's message even though it's never directly spoken.

Reveal the Truth or Make Assumptions

Part of the fun of fiction is when there's subterfuge or when our characters have mistaken assumptions about what's happening.

We can use internal dialogue to show that what our character is saying and what they're feeling inside don't match at all. Internal dialogue allows the reader to know that our character is hiding her emotions, something they couldn't know from the outside.

We can also use internal dialogue to have our character respond in their head to something said aloud, or to jump ahead and make assumptions about what they think the other person will say next.

THE SECRET TO INTERNAL DIALOGUE THAT MOVES THE STORY FORWARD

As you can see, internal dialogue serves many purposes within our story and can move the story forward in multiple ways. But I'd wager that you've also seen internal dialogue that does one of these things and still seems out of place.

The reason is simple.

Internal dialogue should come as a reaction to a prior stimulus. If our internal dialogue doesn't connect directly to what came before it, it will seem random or like the author is intruding to dump in something they think should be there (rather than it being character-driven).

So the not-so-secret secret to internal dialogue that moves the story forward is to check that every passage of internal dialogue comes as a response to something else in the immediate environment.

Now that we've looked at the ways we can use internal dialogue in our stories, we need to consider how we can keep internal dialogue from overwhelming our stories. Even good internal dialogue can be overused or used in problematic proportions compared to external action.

TAKE IT TO THE PAGE

Option A – Quick-Check Version

Step 1 – Select two chapters from different points in your story. Highlight your internal dialogue.

For each section of internal dialogue, label it with either a C (for character), a P (for plot), or an S (for subtle element). If you find you can't apply one of those labels, you need to either remove or rewrite that section of internal dialogue.

Step 2 – Read through one of your chapters. For each passage of internal dialogue, ask yourself this question: Is this internal dialogue a reaction to what came before it?

If so, it can stay. If not, you need to change it or rewrite it so that it does connect to what came before it.

Option B – Full Revision Version

You already have all your passages of internal dialogue highlighted, so they should be easy to find for this exercise as well.

Step 1 – For each section of internal dialogue, label it with either a C (for character), a P (for plot), or an S (for subtle element).

You can use the Comment feature within Microsoft Word to do this if you'd like (and if that's what you're using as your word processing program). Alternatively, you can work backward on this. If you can apply a label, don't leave a comment. If you can't, use the Comment feature to flag that passage for revision.

If you find you can't apply one of those labels, you need to either remove or rewrite that section of internal dialogue.

Step 2 – For each passage of internal dialogue, ask yourself this question: Is this internal dialogue a reaction to what came before it?

If so, it can stay. If not, you need to change it or rewrite it so that it does connect to what came before it.

CHAPTER FIVE

How to Balance Internal Dialogue with External Action

A s fiction writers, we have to walk a fine line. We want to bring the reader close, into the mind of our characters, so that they feel what the characters feel and become emotionally invested in the story. We also need to make sure that we ground them in what's happening outside the character so that they can experience the story as if they were living it.

A story that spends too much time inside the characters starts to feel claustrophobic and as if the story is being told in a big, white void of nothingness. A story that spends too much time outside the characters starts to feel cold and distant. Emotionless.

We have to find the balance between the two.

The first thing we need to do to achieve this balance is to alternate between paragraphs that focus on the point-of-view character and paragraphs that focus on something else.

ALTERNATING THE FOCUS OF PARAGRAPHS

Alternating between paragraphs focused on the POV character and paragraphs focused elsewhere keeps the reader connected to the point-of-view character but doesn't leave them feeling like the character is alone in a black hole. The focus of every paragraph we write should be either on the point-of-view character or on something else. It might sound obvious when I put it that way, but many writers don't do this and don't know they should be doing it. Yet, alternating between the two types of paragraphs is a foundational concept to writing great fiction.

It also helps us answer the question of whether internal dialogue should be set off in its own paragraph or whether it's acceptable to include it in a paragraph along with other elements.

The answer depends on what the paragraph focuses on. So let me explain the two types of paragraphs, and we'll go forward from there.

A paragraph focusing on the point-of-view character can include that character acting, speaking, thinking, or feeling. I call it an internal paragraph because it's coming from inside the point-of-view character and is being projected outward. Much of it will be things (like internal dialogue and emotion) that only the point-of-view character is aware of.

A paragraph that doesn't focus on the point-of-view character will include action done by other characters or action in the environment, dialogue spoken by other characters, or description of the setting or of other characters. I call this an external paragraph because it's happening apart from the point-of-view character. You can tell an external paragraph because it's something that any character in that scene could experience and be aware of. It's public.

We need to alternate between the two. If we have an internal paragraph or two, then we need to make sure we switch to an external paragraph.

As a general guideline, we shouldn't combine the two. Each paragraph we write should be focused on one or the other.

Internal dialogue needs to be placed either in its own paragraph or in a paragraph that focuses on the point-of-view character. If we're writing a paragraph that doesn't focus on the point-of-view character and we now want our next sentence to be a line of internal dialogue, that's when we'd set it off in its own paragraph (or switch to a paragraph that focuses on the point-of-view character).

Because I believe that every concept is easier to understand if we can see an example of it, I'm going to show you what this looks like done both correctly and incorrectly.

The following is the opening of my historical fantasy *The Amazon Heir*, co-written with Lisa Hall-Wilson. The bolded paragraphs are the paragraphs focusing on the external. The italicized paragraphs are focused on the point-of-view character (Kaduis). Internal dialogue is underlined.

> *<u>Kaduis couldn't take pleasure in having women thrown at his feet. Not this day.</u>*
>
> *He swung down from his bay gelding and stalked toward the crowd of Thracians, slaves, and Scythian soldiers gathered on the outskirts of the city to watch and place wagers on the outcome of the negotiations.*
>
> **"A gift." The sun-withered Thracian emissary hauled forward a woman bound at the wrists. "A sample for you, my king, of the excellent slaves we could provide."**
>
> *Kaduis poked a thumb into her mouth and pulled up her lip to inspect her teeth the way he would a horse's. <u>He spent much of his time—too much—meeting with emissaries from</u>*

neighboring peoples wanting a Scythian alliance. Too much time
making war on those who refused to pay the tribute of goods and
flesh his father demanded.

Kaduis ran a hand over the woman's skin to check for sores
or scars and through her honey-colored hair.

"A striking color, is it not, my lord?" the emissary

said. "Very r-rare."

"Not rare enough to raise her value." The lie slipped easily
from his lips after so many years of cheating their allies. "Is this
the best you have to offer?"

He glanced over his shoulder toward the distant outline of the
yurt in the royal quarter where Argotas' wife labored to bring
forth her child. He scowled. If she birthed a boy this time, if his
brother provided their father with the first legitimate male
grandchild—

"Does she not please you?" The emissary crept

forward, eyes lowered. "We have others. Let one of

them warm your bed tonight. You needn't decide r-

right now."

What I want you to notice is how the internal dialogue (underlined) always happens in a paragraph focused on the point-of-view
character (italicized). That's how it should look.

Now let me show you the same passage again. This time I've re-
arranged it so that some of the internal dialogue occurs in a paragraph focused on the external.

Kaduis couldn't take pleasure in having women thrown at his
feet. Not this day.

He swung down from his bay gelding and stalked toward the
crowd of Thracians, slaves, and Scythian soldiers gathered on the
outskirts of the city to watch and place wagers on the outcome of
the negotiations.

"A gift." The sun-withered Thracian emissary

hauled forward a woman bound at the wrists. Kaduis

spent much of his time—too much—meeting with emis-
saries from neighboring peoples wanting a Scythian alliance. Too much time making war on those who
refused to pay the tribute of goods and flesh his father
demanded. **"A sample for you, my king, of the excellent slaves we could provide."**

Let's stop here and pull this apart. We now have what should be
internal dialogue from Kaduis showing up in the middle of a paragraph where the Thracian emissary is speaking and acting (external).

Everything suddenly feels off about this passage. It feels like the
underlined portion in the final paragraph should be internal dialogue belonging to the Thracian, but it's clear it isn't because (1) the
Thracian isn't named but Kaduis is, so we know the Thracian isn't
the point-of-view character, and (2) the Thracian wouldn't know
this about Kaduis, have any reason to think this about Kaduis, or
have any reason to care how Kaduis spends his time.

But it also no longer feels like it belongs to Kaduis. By putting it
in a paragraph where the focus isn't on Kaduis, we've disconnected it
from him. It ends up feeling like author intrusion.

Sometimes, the difference between good internal dialogue and
an author info dump comes down to proper placement.

ADDING VARIETY TO YOUR PARAGRAPHS

Once we're making sure to keep each paragraph focused and to
alternate between the two, we also need to check that the paragraphs
themselves have enough variety. A paragraph that's five sentences of
a character's internal dialogue, for example, will quickly feel stale no
matter how great our internal dialogue is.

One guideline that can help us is one I like to call "less than three, set it free." Yes, it's a silly rhyme, and you don't have to remember it that way if you find it doesn't help you, but I'm a huge fan of memory tricks.

Basically, what this guideline means is that we should try to limit the number of same-type sentences we have in a row to three or fewer. This is true regardless of whether we're writing a paragraph focused on the POV character or a paragraph focused elsewhere.

If we were writing a paragraph focused elsewhere, we might have one sentence of a character acting, and then follow it with two sentences of dialogue.

In a POV character-focused paragraph, we might have a visceral reaction, then a couple lines of internal dialogue, followed by some action and dialogue.

Keep in mind that this is a guideline, not a hard rule, and it's better applied during the editing stage than during the writing stage. When you go back to edit your draft, though, this will help you create paragraphs with enough variety to hold the reader's interest. If you find that a paragraph feels slow or boring and you can't quite put your finger on why, this is one of the first things to check.

CONSIDERATIONS THAT INFLUENCE THE AMOUNT OF INTERNAL DIALOGUE WE USE

The natural question after this would be "Yes, but exactly how much internal dialogue should I use overall? How do I know if I have enough? How do I know if I'm using too much?" Even if we follow the guidelines above, our balance could still be off.

So how do we know if our balance is off and we're either overusing or underusing internal dialogue?

The first answer is that it depends in part on the conventions of our genre and the narrative heat and distance readers of that genre expect. A romance will use more internal dialogue overall than will a thriller, for example. One of the most beneficial exercises you can do is to pick two or three of the best books in your genre and carefully study how much internal dialogue they use. I know that might seem tedious, but if you're going to appeal to readers of a particular genre, you need to give them what they want. (This is the exercise I recommended in Chapter One's Take It to the Page section.)

The second answer is the topic of our next chapter: Clues We're Overusing or Underusing Internal Dialogue.

TAKE IT TO THE PAGE

Option A – Quick-Check Version

Step 1 – Select two chapters from different places in your manuscript. Use two different colors to highlight your paragraphs based on their focus. I like to change the text color instead because it makes it easier to read, and I use red for paragraphs focused on the point-of-view character and blue for paragraphs focused elsewhere.

Step 2 – Read through these chapters slowly, looking at where each passage of internal dialogue lies. Ask yourself these questions:

Does each passage of internal dialogue show up in a paragraph either by itself or focused on the point-of-view character?

Do I have long sections where I don't swap my focus often enough?

Option B – Full Revision Version

Step 1 – Highlight all paragraphs that don't focus on your point-of-view character. (I like to change the text color instead.)

Step 2 – Look at your highlighted paragraphs of internal dialogue.

Does each passage of internal dialogue show up in a paragraph either by itself or focused on the point-of-view character?

Do you have long sections where you don't swap your focus often enough?

CHAPTER SIX

Clues We're Overusing or Underusing Internal Dialogue

When I receive a manuscript for editing from a new client, I can tell within the first few pages whether they're going to struggle with internal dialogue and whether their biggest problem is going to be overusing it or underusing it. It's rare for an author to overuse internal dialogue in one scene but underuse it in another. We usually have a problem one way or the other. Once you identify which way you might accidentally lean, it'll help you during self-editing to start fixing your bad habits.

I'll start with the clues that we might be overusing internal dialogue.

Overuse Clue #1 – We're repeating the same thing in internal dialogue as we're also showing in dialogue or action.

Each sentence we write should introduce something new to the story. It's the concept of *everything in fiction needs to be there for a reason and needs to move the story forward.* When we repeat ourselves, in any fashion, it doesn't move the story forward.

So, for example, if we use internal dialogue to show a character thinking about how she wants to cry or how she wants to slap the person who stole her job, and then we show her crying or show her slapping, our internal dialogue and action overlap.

What we want to do instead is to use one or the other (not both) or to add some variety to either the internal dialogue or action. Continuing with our example above, perhaps our character wants to cry, but she's been told her whole life that crying is weak. We could have her express her deep sadness in a different way, such as cracking open a chocolate bar, throwing something, or delving into what that sadness feels like throughout the rest of her body when she holds it in.

Or we could add variety by showing that the way our character imagined something happening is very different from the way it actually happens. Perhaps in her internal dialogue, she thinks about how good it will feel to slap him, but when she does, both her hand and her heart end up hurting.

It might seem obvious, but we also shouldn't double up on what's said in internal dialogue and in spoken dialogue. You'd be surprised how often I see something like this...

Who did he think she was, Houdini? She didn't know how to pick a lock. "I don't know how to pick a lock."

The fix for this involves us deciding where that dialogue actually needs to be—inside or outside. Look at our example again with a simple fix...

> Who did he think she was, Houdini? "I don't know how to pick a lock."

Repetitious internal dialogue makes for boring, flabby reading. This first clue could also mean that we're not using internal dialogue to its best advantage, rather than that we're simply overusing internal dialogue. Use this clue in conjunction with the other overuse clues to decide whether you're actually overusing internal dialogue or whether you simply need to take better advantage of the internal dialogue you have.

Overuse Clue #2 – We have as much internal dialogue during a tense action scene as we do during a quieter reaction scene.

In the previous chapter, I explained how we need to alternate between paragraphs focused on the point-of-view character and paragraphs focused elsewhere. That's true regardless of whether we're writing a fast-paced action scene or a slower-paced reaction scene where the character is digesting their latest failure and trying to come up with a new plan.

The difference comes in how much space we devote to each. When we want a scene to feel fast-paced, we need to use less internal dialogue overall and shorter, sharper point-of-view character-focused paragraphs. Within those POV character-focused paragraphs, we should use more visceral hits (how their body instinctively reacts to what's around them) than internal dialogue. We don't have as much time to think when our life is in danger or when we need to make quick decisions to prevent something bad from happening.

If you find that you're using the same amount of internal dialogue in what should be a fast-paced action scene, it could be a clue that you're overusing internal dialogue.

One of the main causes for this is if we haven't laid the groundwork well enough prior to this scene. In other words, we're partway into our fast-paced scene and we realize that the reader doesn't yet know a key piece of information. We start adding to the scene to make sure the reader isn't confused. Fast-paced action scenes aren't the place for that. If we figure out we're missing some foundational pieces, we should backtrack and add as many of them as we can prior to the action.

Overuse Clue #3 – We're using internal dialogue to sum up our scene at the end or forecast what's coming before the scene starts.

I suspect that our tendency to do this comes from our school days. Teachers taught us to write introductions and conclusions to our essays, and it's a habit we struggle to break when it comes to writing a scene.

Summing up our scenes at the end or forecasting what's coming before the scene starts also happen for others reasons. When we forecast through internal dialogue, we're often hoping to hook the reader. When we sum up our scenes at the end, we're often hoping to remind them of what's just happened so they'll carry it with them into the next scene.

Neither are necessary. Both indicate that we're overusing internal dialogue, and it's time to make some hard cuts.

Before I move on to the next point, I want to clarify the difference between foreshadowing and forecasting. Some writers think that what they're doing is foreshadowing when in reality it's forecasting.

Foreshadowing is a good thing. In foreshadowing, you drop subtle hints for the reader of what might be coming in the future (e.g., your main character notices something just in passing that becomes important later in the story, or you show your main character's ability to tie knots and that ability will be crucial in the climax). In forecasting, you tell the reader what's coming.

Overuse Clue #4 – Within our internal dialogue, we're repeating the same idea in multiple ways.

Of all the overuse clues, repeating the same idea in multiple ways can be the trickiest to spot because it's a balance issue. It's easy to confuse with developing a character's internal situation during an important moment.

Here's what I mean by that. When something extremely important happens to our point-of-view character, we need to spend more time on their reaction to it.

Where we often stumble, though, is that each sentence in that reaction needs to show progress rather than wallowing in the same ideas, phrased differently. Allow me to show you an example.

> How could he have done this to her? She felt like she was trapped in a bad remake of *Shallow Hal* where it turned out Hal didn't care about Rosemary after all. Only the lowest level of slimeball pretended to be someone's friend just to get a leg-up on a promotion at work. It was as bad as dating the boss's daughter to get ahead. Using any kind of relationship for the sole purpose of bettering yourself in a job was unethical.

Are you tired of hearing the character think about this yet? When we don't introduce anything fresh, the reader quickly finds the character's thoughts boring. It's like when someone tells you the same story every time you talk to them. After a while, you cringe inside when you know they're about to start up again and you tune them out.

Don't let this example lull you into a false sense of security, though. Maybe we don't have our character think about the same thing in different ways within a single paragraph, but we have them think about the same thing at different times.

For example, let's say we have a character who thinks her husband might have lied to her. In Scene A, we show her thinking about how she feels about that and deciding what to do about it. Then in Scene D, she's in a different physical situation, but we have her thinking about how she feels about his potential lies again. Then we show it again in Scene E.

If she's thinking about the same thing without making progress in either her emotions toward the situation or how she wants to handle the situation, or in finding evidence to either prove or disprove that he did lie to her, then we're overusing internal dialogue. Your character can think about the same event, but each instance of internal dialogue needs to show progress of some kind.

Many of us will need to depend on critique partners, beta readers, and editors to point this overuse out to us.

Overuse Clue #5 – Every paragraph focused on the POV character includes internal dialogue.

Not every paragraph that focuses on the point-of-view character needs to include internal dialogue. Not every line of dialogue by the POV character needs to be preceded or broken up by internal dialogue. If you have a large chunk of internal dialogue in every other paragraph, that can be a clue that you're overusing it.

Now that you've seen the clues that you might be overusing internal dialogue, we need to look at the clues that you might be *under*using it.

Underuse Clue #1 – It's not clear to a reader *why* our character is acting the way they are.

In other words, if our character's motivations aren't clear, we might be underusing internal dialogue.

We already looked at using internal dialogue to develop motivation in the chapter on how to use internal dialogue to move the story forward. I gave some examples there of times when a writer lost me as a reader because I didn't understand a character's actions. This is simply the flip side of that coin.

The motivation could be that what just happened caused an emotional reaction, it could be a snippet of memory triggered by what's happening to them, or it could be that they're rationally putting the puzzle pieces together and coming to a conclusion about what needs to be done. The bottom line is that readers want to know the *why* behind our character's actions.

Underuse Clue #2 – Our point-of-view character receives a major revelation and doesn't process it in their mind. Or something happens to our point-of-view character that would hurt them, confuse them, make them conflicted, or otherwise arise emotions in a normal person, and our character doesn't react internally.

In real life, how we act is always a reaction to a trigger. A stimulus/motivation/cause results in a reaction/effect. This natural chain of actions and reactions is even more true and necessary within fiction. If you skip a reaction, your point-of-view character can end up feeling flat or robotic.

Reactions don't always have to include internal dialogue, but internal dialogue is often a key element in important reactions because it's how we, as human beings, process what's happening to us.

TAKE IT TO THE PAGE

Option A – Quick-Check Version

What you're looking to do is learn whether you're prone to overusing or underusing internal dialogue. This doesn't mean you'll never overuse internal dialogue if you tend to underuse it, but it does help you identify your weaknesses.

Take these steps and it should point you in the right direction.

Step 1 – Pick a scene you intended to be a fast-paced action scene from your book and one you meant to be a slower-paced reaction scene. Highlight the internal dialogue in both. Does the same pattern appear, or can you see the difference?

Step 2 – Quickly check the beginning and ending paragraphs of each of your scenes. Are you forecasting? If so, delete it.

Step 3 – Take one of the scenes you highlighted earlier to show the paragraphs focused on the POV character and the paragraphs focused elsewhere. Does each paragraph focused on the POV character use internal dialogue?

Step 4 – Choose a few chapters where your character has a major revelation or takes a major emotional hit. Do they react to it in internal dialogue?

Option B – Full Revision Version

Step 1 – Compare your fast-paced action scenes to your slower-paced scenes. Are you using the same amount of internal dialogue in each? This should be easy to see since you've highlighted your passages of internal dialogue. If you are, work on trimming out any unnecessary internal dialogue in the scenes that are meant to be faster-paced.

Step 2 – Quickly check the beginning and ending paragraphs of each of your scenes. Are you forecasting? If so, delete it.

Step 3 – Check if you're using internal dialogue in almost every paragraph that focuses on your point-of-view character. This should be easy to see since you've already color-coded your passages in the previous chapter. If you see that you have internal dialogue in almost every paragraph that focuses on your POV character, you're probably over-using internal dialogue.

Step 4 – Copy and paste (in order) all the spots where your character is thinking about the same thing and make note of what page that selection came from. Read it over. This will quickly show you if there's progress in her thoughts or if she's basically running on a mouse wheel and getting nowhere.

Step 5 – Look at the passages where your character has a major revelation or takes a major emotional hit. Do they react to it? Is their reaction in proportion to whatever caused it?

Bonus Step – When you eventually ask a friend, critique partner, beta reader, or editor to read your manuscript, make sure to ask them to mark any spot where they aren't sure *why* your character is acting the way they are.

CHAPTER SEVEN

Using Questions In Internal Dialogue: A Unique Challenge

The second most frequently asked question about internal dialogue (after formatting) seems to be whether or not we should use questions within our internal dialogue.

Writers are often told they shouldn't. Too many questions used in internal dialogue can come across as lazy, weak writing. Used strategically, however, questions in internal dialogue can deepen your point of view and enhance the emotion, tension, and realistic feel. We do ask ourselves questions. (Some of us even answer them.)

The truth is that there's no hard ruling one way or another about questions in internal dialogue. As with most writing techniques, you need balance.

GOOD REASONS TO USE INTERNAL QUESTIONS

As we go through these good reasons to use internal questions, keep in mind what I mentioned above about balance. Even good things can become a problem when used in excess.

So how can we use questions in internal dialogue to our advantage?

To punctuate a character's emotions through (mostly) rhetorical questions.

What falls into this category are the questions we'd naturally say when we're upset. Sometimes a character will say these things out loud, but they'll just as often keep these responses to themselves.

Is she serious?

How could he do this to me?

Are you insane?

We don't usually expect to seek an answer to these questions. They can also be a good way of showing that what a character is thinking doesn't match up with what they're saying.

To show a character figuring something out.

Questions in internal dialogue can help when a character is putting previous pieces together to find a connection or they're making a supposition (a guess or logical leap) without enough information to prove they're right.

For example...

Jessie walked the room again, feeling like she was trying to unravel a magician's secrets. Only two men had the combination to the safe where the artifact was kept, and you couldn't even enter the code without fingerprint recognition. A fingerprint match unlocked the keypad.

She stopped beside Keith's desk and picked up a framed photograph of Keith and Dr. Matthews in dig gear. Keith had an unbreakable alibi for the time range of the theft, and last she checked, ghosts couldn't open safes. Could Dr. Matthews have faked his own death?

Internal dialogue questions work in these situations because it's a way we naturally use internal questions in real life. We make intuitive leaps by asking ourselves questions and by questioning our previous assumptions.

To reinforce the scene or story goal or as a reminder of what's at stake if the goal isn't reached.

Internal questions act almost as a highlighter by suggesting that the answers to these questions are important.

Where could he have hidden the gun?

If she didn't find a new job soon, how was she going to pay her rent?

Using internal questions in this way is very "on the nose," so we need to consider whether the reader needs the reminder/clear statement or whether we're just beating it into them with a stick.

To strengthen a character's sarcastic nature.

Earlier on, we looked at using internal dialogue to aid in characterization. One way we can do that is to use questions in internal dialogue to show that a character is sarcastic.

I'll show you an example from earlier where the character's personality came through as biting or sarcastic.

Who did he think she was, Houdini? "I don't know how to pick a lock."

This could as easily have been played straight.

If she'd had the time, maybe she could have learned via YouTube videos, but now... "I don't know how to pick a lock."

That internal dialogue doesn't use a question and shows us a very different character reaction. This second character seriously considers what's been said.

To show an I'm-trying-to-convince-myself denial of what the character knows to be true or to show the character debating with themselves.

Internal dialogue can help build conflict within a character as they try to decide on their next step. It can also show a character who's clearly lying to themselves or who doesn't want to face the truth.

For example...

It wasn't really stealing, right? Not if he planned to pay it back?

These moments feel authentic because we've all experienced those situations where we've talked ourselves into—or out of—something.

To increase tension, conflict, or emotional upheaval.

This one walks a fine line because it can be overdone more easily than the others. One way you can think of these internal questions is as your character's way of trying to process something that hits them so deeply that they don't yet know how to deal with it.

Let's say we have a thriller where the villain is actually a vigilante trying to expose the horrible and irreparable side effects of a weight loss drug a pharmaceutical company has managed to fast-track onto the market. The side effect is extremely rare at normal dosage levels, but his wife suffered from it. No one listened to him when he tried to go through official channels to have the drug removed from the market. Now he's decided to inject an overdose of the drug into high-ranking officials until someone listens to him.

Our point-of-view character has just been injected.

> Her body ached deep down in her bones, at the core of her joints. Every step became a new lesson in agony. She stumbled and grabbed onto the stair railing. He'd claimed his wife wasn't the only one. How many? How could they live through even one day feeling like this?

REASONS TO REMOVE YOUR INTERNAL QUESTIONS

When it's redundant.

Redundancy happens when we repeat something in our internal dialogue that we've already written in narrative, action, or spoken dialogue. We talked about redundancy (or repetition) in our overuse clues, so I won't be redundant myself by belaboring the point.

When a series of internal questions creates a repetitious feel to your writing.

Any pattern that we overuse can become a problem.

She peeked through her kitchen window. The lieutenant stood at her door. What was he doing here? Had he come to arrest her? What kind of sentence did the courts give for trespassing?

These rapid-gunfire questions are also a problem because they don't allow the character a chance to develop any of those thoughts in-depth. They become a surface skim of the situation, which can make our internal dialogue feel emotionless and rushed.

When it feels like the obvious thing to ask in that situation.

If the reader is already going to be asking themselves a specific question, you usually don't need to put it on the page.

Kate sidestepped the pool of blood that had spread out in a nearly perfect circle underneath the dead man hanging from the ceiling. Antiques lay shattered along the gallery walls, and the multi-million dollar modern art piece the local paper had recently highlighted bore three long slashes, like a tiger ran his claws down it. What had happened here?

Because this question doesn't add anything new, it's wasted space. Internal questions, just like everything in internal dialogue, need to move the story forward.

When it's there to tell the reader what question they should be asking.

At the opposite end of the spectrum from questions that don't need to be there because they're too obvious are questions whose sole purpose for existence is to lead the reader by the hand.

Let me break that down for you a bit. If you remember our definition of internal dialogue, internal dialogue is a character thinking to *themselves*. In other words, an internal question shouldn't be put on the page solely for the reader's sake. When you use an internal question solely for the reader's sake, it's a sneaky form of author intrusion.

Sometimes we can fall into this trap because we want to make sure the reader's mind is going down the right path. It's almost like we're saying "See? Get it?"

We might also fall into this trap if we haven't put enough information into the story itself for the reader to ever reach the conclusion we want them to reach. Usually this happens because we've skipped some steps somewhere and now we need to find a way to make the reader ask questions they wouldn't have otherwise been asking themselves.

In either of those situations, the internal questions we're using will come across as awkward and out of place.

I recommend not worrying about how many internal questions you use in your first draft. Come back later and assess whether you really need those questions or whether you can write the same thing in a better way.

TAKE IT TO THE PAGE

Both option paths come together for this Take It to the Page because we can use the Find feature in our word processing program to help us quickly locate internal questions.

Simply open the Advanced Find box and add a question mark. Click Find Next.

Along with showing you internal questions, this will show you questions in dialogue. You can skip those.

When you reach an internal dialogue question, ask yourself whether it does one of these things:

- Does it punctuate a character's emotions through (mostly) rhetorical questions?
- Does it show a character figuring something out or making an intuitive leap?
- Does it reinforce the scene or story goal, or serve as a reminder of what's at stake if the goal isn't reached?
- Does it show that your character is sarcastic in nature?
- Does it show an I'm-trying-to-convince-myself denial of what the character knows to be true or the character debating with themselves?
- Does it increase tension, conflict, or emotional upheaval?

If it doesn't do one of these things, odds are you can safely remove it and you won't lose anything.

For the questions that remain, ask yourself if there's a different way you could write it that would still clearly deliver the message or the same impact. If so, rewrite it.

Internal Dialogue, Internal Monologue, Soliloquy, and Other Terms

We can resolve a lot of the confusion when it comes to writing if we take the time to define terms when talking about a subject. In the first chapter of this book, I explained the difference between internal dialogue and narration, but a host of other terms are at least loosely related to the concept of character thoughts—stream of consciousness, soliloquy, inner dialogue, internal dialogue, and internal monologue.

Stream of Consciousness

Internal dialogue and stream of consciousness both give you the point-of-view character's thoughts, but internal dialogue does it in small, structured, clear snippets. The laws of cause and effect and action and reaction bind internal dialogue, and as writers, we should only use it to advance the plot. Internal dialogue serves as one part of a much larger equation of description, emotion, setting, action, etc. You'll find internal dialogue in all genres and in both literary and commercial fiction.

Stream of consciousness is more a style of writing—a genre in itself.

Stream of consciousness writing seeks to mimic in its entirety the chaotic, random, sometimes purposeless thoughts that fly through the human brain all day long. This doesn't mean that stream of consciousness writing is without meaning. In the midst of the messiness of the human mind, patterns and meaning do emerge, and so, likewise, they rise to the surface in stream of consciousness writing.

But stream of consciousness writing doesn't appeal to everyone. Much of the time, the reader has to work hard to figure out what's going on. There's more ambiguity. The plot (when there is one) isn't always linear because the way human beings process information and memories isn't always linear.

You'll often find that writers use stream of consciousness writing to recreate a mental state that would be difficult to authentically replicate in any other form. Examples of this include mental illness, drug-induced states, hallucinations, and comas.

If you'd like to become more familiar with this style of writing, take a look at William Faulkner's *The Sound and the Fury*, James Joyce's *Ulysses*, Samuel Backett's *Molloy*, Jack Kerouac's *On the Road*, and Marcel Proust's *Remembrance of Things Past*.

Soliloquy

A soliloquy is when a character speaks his or her thoughts out loud, regardless of any listeners. The character might be alone or there might be other characters around (or an audience). You most often see this in plays, with the classic example being Hamlet's "To be or not to be" speech.

The main difference between internal dialogue and a soliloquy is that the former is internal and the latter is external. Internal dialogue is meant to be private, while a soliloquy is ambivalent. The speaker doesn't care if it's heard or not.

You won't often see a soliloquy in novels or short stories, and with good reason. It's strange and/or annoying when someone speaks their private thoughts aloud for any length of time. In prose fiction, it can also feel very unnatural.

Sometimes we can use a single line of soliloquy to good effect, but if we're going to try this, we need to be careful to make it seem natural. For example, you might have a woman in a grocery store, who's reading her list rather than watching where she's going and bumps into a tower of tomato soup cans, knocking them over. Out loud, she might say something like...

"Idiot!"

Or...

"That was stupid."

Or...

"Why am I so clumsy all the time?"

Those exclamations are actually her thoughts spoken aloud. They're a short soliloquy.

Another example of when you might use a soliloquy would be if you have a character alone in a tight spot. Many of us, when we're under extreme pressure, give ourselves a pep talk.

Imagine you have a character who was pushed over the edge of a cliff and left for dead by your villain. She managed to grab onto a tree root rather than plummeting to her death, and has been inching her way up the cliff ever since. Her arms are shaking, and she's starting to get dizzy from dehydration. She might say something out loud to herself like...

> "You can do this. You ran a marathon. You had a baby without any drugs. This is nothing compared to that. Just a few more feet."

Or imagine you have a character who's trying to defuse a bomb as the timer ticks down. He might say something to himself like...

> "Red or blue? Red or blue? Which one do they always cut on TV?"

If you're going to use a soliloquy in your fiction, use it wisely and remember that, since it's basically internal dialogue spoken aloud, all the same rules apply.

Inner Dialogue, Internal Dialogue, and Internal Monologue

For the most part, when you read about inner dialogue, internal dialogue, or internal monologue, the writers all mean the same thing. Inner dialogue and internal dialogue always mean the same thing.

In her class on internal dialogue, however, my friend Lisa Hall-Wilson pointed out that we could actually distinguish between internal dialogue and internal monologue if we wanted to.

Before I explain the difference, I want to remind you that, when we, as writers, talk about internal dialogue, we usually use it as an umbrella term to mean both internal dialogue and internal monologue. Consequently, when you read a book, article, or blog post talking about internal dialogue, you should assume the author means both internal dialogue and internal monologue unless they specifically state otherwise.

But sometimes, when we're thinking about how we want to use that voice inside our character's head, it can be useful to break it down into internal dialogue and internal monologue.

Internal monologue is a one-sided, running commentary with yourself. It's unidirectional. Think of it more like a speech to a crowd of one than like a conversation.

> I wish I hadn't worn a skirt and heels. They should have told us ahead of time that part of this conference would include a team-building hike.

For most of us, internal monologue is an accepted part of our life. It's also going to be the most common type of internal "speech" used in our fiction. We naturally react to and analyze what's happening around us through our internal monologue.

Internal dialogue is talking to yourself. It's more of a back and forth, some of which can be spoken aloud. I'll give you a couple of examples to show you how it can work with both dialogue spoken to other characters and soliloquy. I'll start with soliloquy.

> Melinda reached for her cell phone. Her hand caught air instead. "Where would I have left it? I had it when I came home last night?" She turned in a tight circle. It wasn't on the dining room table. The chair! "I bet it fell out of my pocket last night."

In this example, no one is with Melinda. She's asking herself questions, answering them in her head, and then speaking out loud to herself again. It's a back and forth, but she's the only one involved. If you're not sure whether or not to use this type of internal dialogue, ask yourself whether you'd use internal dialogue in this way if you were in the same situation as your character.

You could also use this as an element of characterization. Perhaps you have a character who feels overlooked and ignored, and so she's taken up the habit of talking to herself in this way because it makes her feel listened to.

The more common type of internal dialogue, though, is when we intend for our spoken dialogue to be heard by another person, but we also have a secret "conversation" or response with ourselves in our heads.

> Melinda rounded the corner and ran into a broad chest. The man attached to it stumbled backward and caught himself just before bumping into the red velvet rope surrounding the sculpture created entirely from recycled soda cans.
>
> Her gaze connected with his and her apology died on her lips. "What are you doing here, Jake?" *Other than spying on me for your brother.* "I thought you hated modern art."

This type of internal dialogue is fantastic for conveying the personality of your point-of-view character or for adding tension or humor to a scene.

Even though we don't normally distinguish between the types of internal dialogue and internal monologue when talking about the topic, knowing that these different types exist can help us add much-needed variety to the internal speech in our writing.

Head-Hopping vs. Omniscient POV

Before I dive in to explaining the difference between head-hopping and omniscient point of view, we need to get one thing out of the way.

Head-hopping is never good. Sometimes an author can get away with it, but it's never ideal and it never makes your story stronger. Never.

Omniscient point of view, on the other hand, is a valid point of view for fiction. It might not be the most popular or the most commonly used in twenty-first-century fiction, but there's nothing wrong with it. And some stories are even best told in it.

Obviously, the tricky part for writers is telling them apart. I'm going to show you the secret for keeping them straight.

When we talk about point of view (POV), we basically mean the point of view from which the story is told. Who are you listening to? Whose head are you in? In a practical sense, POV lays the foundation for everything you'll write in your story, and it comes in four types. One of those types is omniscient.

Omniscient POV is when the story is told by an all-knowing narrator. That all-knowing narrator is the author, and the story is told in his or her voice rather than in any particular character's voice. (For an excellent example of how to write omniscient POV well, check out Rachel Aaron's *The Spirit Thief*.)

To be head-hopping, a passage needs to meet two criteria:

1. The viewpoint shifts between characters without a proper transition (e.g., a scene break).
2. The thoughts/feelings of the characters are given in their voices rather than in the author's voice.

Now that you know the definition of head-hopping, you'll be able to run everything through its filter to decide if a passage is head-hopping or genuinely omniscient POV.

Omniscient POV will be written in the author's voice. The characters' feelings and thoughts will be filtered through the author narrator.

Head-hopping will be in the characters' voices, and you'll go back and forth without a proper transition.

Let me give you an example of head-hopping so you can see it in action...

> Jack rolled down the window half an inch, a smirk spreading across his face. The slut would never find her way back without him, and no one would find her until the coyotes had picked her bones clean.
>
> Anna yanked at the door handle. Her chest felt heavy, her lungs unwilling to suck in a full breath. "Unlock the door, Jake. This isn't funny anymore."
>
> Jake's cold blue eyes stared into hers. After all she'd made him suffer through, he was going to enjoy this moment. Savor it like a medium-rare T-bone steak.

Now let's break it apart.

Jack rolled down the window half an inch, a smirk spreading across his face. – Sounds like we're in someone else's POV here. Someone who's watching Jake. If we were in Jake's POV, this would read *Jake rolled down the window half an inch and smirked.*

The slut would never find her way back without him, and no one would find her until the coyotes had picked her bones clean. – We're hearing Jake's thoughts in Jake's voice. It's him, not the author, thinking of Anna as a slut.

Anna yanked at the door handle. Her chest felt heavy, her lungs unwilling to suck in a full breath. – Now we're firmly in Anna's head. Only she can describe how her chest feels and the dread settling there.

"Unlock the door, Jake. This isn't funny anymore."

Jake's cold blue eyes stared into hers. – Still in Anna's POV since she's the one who can see Jake's eye color.

After all she'd made him suffer through, he was going to enjoy this moment. Savor it like a rare T-bone steak. – Jake's thoughts in Jake's voice again.

Head-hopping damages your story because it makes the writing feel choppy. Readers constantly need to pause, however slightly, and figure out who they're supposed to identify with. They're often left feeling disconnected entirely. Even if they don't know what to call head-hopping, they'll know something is off and that they have a difficult time connecting emotionally with the characters/narrator. Readers need to connect emotionally with either the characters (in first-person POV and third-person POV) or with the author narrator (in omniscient POV).

Showing and Telling in Fiction

The following excerpts come from my book *Showing and Telling in Fiction*. Because I know that not everyone who reads this book will have also read that one, I decided it would help to include a bit about the topic here, specifically in how it relates to internal dialogue.

WHAT DO WE MEAN BY SHOWING?

Showing happens when we let the reader experience things for themselves, through the perspective of the characters. Jeff Gerke, former owner of Marcher Lord Press, explains showing in one simple question: Can the camera see it?[2]

While I love that way of looking at it, we'd really have to ask can the camera see it, hear it, smell it, touch it, taste it, or think it? (And

---

[2] Jeff Gerke, *The First 50 Pages* (Cincinnati: Writer's Digest Books, 2011), 40.

that would be a strange camera.) Because of that, I prefer to think about showing as being in a *Star Trek* holodeck.

For those of you who aren't as nerdy as I am, a holodeck is a virtual reality room where users can act as a character in a story, which is fully projected using photons and force fields. You can play Jane Eyre or *Twilight*'s Bella or Lee Child's Jack Reacher.

What the user experiences is what they can see, hear, touch, taste, or smell. In holodecks, you can smell things and you can eat or drink "replicated" food. It's a completely immersive experience. To the holodeck user, the experience seems real in all respects. And if you turn the holodeck safety systems off, you can be injured or even die.

When you're faced with deciding whether something is showing or telling, ask yourself this question: If this were a holodeck program, would I be able to experience this?

Let's take a couple examples and test them out. A straightforward one first.

Kate realized she'd locked her keys in the car.

Now, you're standing in the holodeck. What do you experience? ...Nothing. We can't see "realized." We don't know how she knows her keys are locked in the car. Anything we might visualize is something we've had to add because the author didn't. There's no picture here.

Here's one possible showing version...

Kate yanked on the car door handle. The door didn't budge, and her keys dangled from the ignition. "Dang it!"

You don't have to tell us Kate realized her keys were locked inside her car because we're right there with her. We see her figure it out.

Let's take a more challenging example. This time you're in the holodeck, playing the character of Linda. (Remember that, since you're Linda, you can hear her thoughts, as well as see, smell, hear, taste, and feel what she does.)

First the "telling" version.

> Linda stood at the edge of the Grand Canyon. Though her head spun from the height, she was amazed by the grandeur of it and felt a sense of excitement. Finally she'd taken a big step toward overcoming her fear of heights.

What do you physically experience in the holodeck? Only the Grand Canyon. If you don't know what the Grand Canyon looks like, you can't see even that. None of the rest can appear around you. None of it is her thoughts. They're all abstractions. What does being amazed by the grandeur look like? What does excitement feel like? What does her fear of heights feel like?

If we're in the holodeck, it's going to play out something more like this...

> Linda gripped the damp metal railing that ringed the horseshoe-shaped walkway over the Grand Canyon. Her vision blurred, and she drew in a deep breath and puffed it out the way the instructor taught her in Lamaze class. If it worked for childbirth, it should work to keep her from passing out now. She forced her gaze down to the glass floor. Thick bands of rust red and tan alternated their way down canyon walls that looked as if they'd been chiseled by a giant sculptor. The shaking in her legs faded. She had to get a picture to take back to her kids.

You can see what's around Linda, and you sense her amazement at the size of the canyon, as well as feel her fear. Emotionally you move with her from fear to wonder to excitement as she thinks about sharing it with her children. We hear it in her thoughts. This is the trick to good internal dialogue. It's what your character is thinking at that moment, the way they would think it. It's like you've planted a listening device in their brain and can play their thoughts on a speaker.

So the next time you're not sure whether you're showing or telling, ask "What would I experience in a holodeck?" That's how you should write it if you want to show rather than tell.

WHAT IS TELLING?

The simple answer would be to say that telling is everything that's not showing, but that's not exact enough for me. What I like to do is compare telling and showing when defining telling.

If showing presents evidence to the reader and allows them to draw their own conclusions, telling dictates a conclusion to the reader, telling them what to believe. It states a fact.

Bob was angry…dictates a conclusion.

But what was the evidence?

Bob punched his fist into the wall.

The Black Plague ravaged the country…dictates a conclusion.

But what was the evidence?

You could describe men loading dead bodies covered in oozing black sores onto a wagon. Your protagonist could press a handkerchief filled with posies to her nose and mouth as she passes someone who's drawing in ragged, labored breaths.

Either of those details, or many others, would show the Black Death ravaging the country.

REALIZED OR *WONDERED* AS THOUGHTS

The words *realized* and *wondered* can be an indicator that you're telling the reader the point of view character is realizing or wondering rather than showing them realize or showing them wonder.

Remember this example from when we talked about the holodeck?

> *Telling*: Kate <u>realized</u> she'd locked her keys inside the car.

> *Showing*: Kate yanked on the car door handle. The door didn't budge, and her keys dangled from the ignition. "Dang it!"

The word *realized* should now be a red flag to you that you might be telling.

> *Telling*: She disappeared around the corner. Robert <u>wondered</u> if he'd ever see her again.

> *Showing*: She disappeared around the corner. Would he ever see her again?

In the telling version, you the author are telling us what Robert wondered. In the showing version, you're hearing Robert's internal dialogue. In essence, you're showing his thoughts.

There are times when *realized* and *wondered* don't necessarily mean you're telling (usually when you're writing in a first-person POV). Context serves as the deciding factor.

For example...

> I realized I was being difficult, but I didn't care.

If we're in first person point of view, there's no other way the narrator can convey to the reader that they're aware of their actions yet indifferent to any problem those actions might cause.

Other, similar words that could potentially indicate telling and that you should watch for are...

Thought
Knew
Remembered
Recalled
Reviewed
Considered

These won't always indicate telling, but they can. They're all similar in that they're all about what's happening in the character's head, and they all add distance. When in doubt, look at the word in the context of the surrounding passage.

How to Use Tags in Internal Dialogue

When it comes to tags, internal dialogue thought tags are formatted in almost the exact same way as spoken dialogue tags.

Use a comma at the end of a segment of internal dialogue (even a complete sentence) when followed by a tag. A tag is a word such as *thought* or *wondered*.

I wish I'd packed the GPS, she thought.

Use a question mark without a comma for a question. This applies to exclamation marks too.

Does he even know where we're going? she wondered.

Not a chance! he thought.

If a tag is dividing a sentence, use a comma at the end of the first section of internal dialogue (even if the comma wouldn't normally go there in the same sentence if it wasn't internal dialogue) and use a comma after the tag.

The next time we plan a long trip, she thought, *I'm going to navigate instead of leaving it up to chance.*

Use a period after a tag when the first segment of internal dialogue is a complete sentence.

He'll never admit he doesn't know where we are, she thought. *We could be lost for days at this rate.*

Use a dash when internal dialogue is cut off or interrupted. Do not add any other punctuation.

If I'd been allowed to—
"I know what you're thinking." He wiped a palm across his dusty forehead. "And you're wrong."

Use an ellipsis for internal dialogue that fades away.

Basic needs first. We're going to need food, shelter, water... A shiver crawled up her legs and buried itself in the pit of her stomach. They weren't going to survive this.

Use exclamation marks sparingly! Sometimes you need an exclamation point to add emotional context, but they're usually a sign that you're trying to bolster weak internal dialogue. They're also distracting!! And if you use them too often, they lose their emphasis!!

Don't use colons or semicolons in your internal dialogue at all. While this might seem like an arbitrary rule, colons and semicolons just look unnatural in internal dialogue. For the most part, you should avoid them in your fiction entirely. The old joke is that you're allowed one semicolon per career, so use it wisely.

Take It to the Page for Full Revision

The full revision option requires a lot of highlighting. You can do this by printing out a paper copy and using three differently colored highlighters, but I like to use the highlight and change-font-color options in my word processing program. This saves paper. It also saves me headaches when I want to change something. Changes made on printed paper are permanent.

Because you'll be making a lot of changes to your file, I strongly recommend that you save the file you'll be working on as a separate document. This preserves your original. (I actually recommend that authors save their manuscript as a new version for every major revision.)

Highlight all your good internal dialogue passages in one color and highlight all your bad indirect internal dialogue passages in another. (I suggest using yellow and green.)

Now change the font color on the rest of your document. Pick one font color for paragraphs that focus on your point-of-view character and another font color for paragraphs focused elsewhere. (I like red for POV character-focused paragraphs and blue for paragraphs focused elsewhere.)

We're now ready to start revising.

You'll notice that this list seems out of order compared to the chapters in this book. That's because the way the chapters needed to be organized to teach about internal dialogue aren't necessarily also the best order for self-editing your internal dialogue. This is one of the reasons I strongly recommended that those of you undertaking a full revision should use this Take It to the Page full list instead.

Chapter Two Exercises – Fixing Bad Indirect Internal Dialogue

We need to start with fixing any bad indirect internal dialogue.

Since you've highlighted good and bad internal dialogue in separate colors, bad indirect internal dialogue should be easy to find.

For each passage of bad indirect internal dialogue, ask yourself if this section of internal dialogue is really important.

If so, try rewriting it using a mixture of direct and indirect internal dialogue. If not, try rewriting it using good indirect internal dialogue.

Not sure if you've succeeded?

Try these tests:

1. Take your indirect internal dialogue and rewrite it in first person. Good indirect internal dialogue should sound smooth and natural when you change it from third person to first person. That's because internal dialogue is the character thinking to themselves.

2. Read the internal dialogue out loud. Could you imagine yourself saying these things? Does it read smoothly, or do you stumble over it?

Chapter Six Exercises

The next piece of the process is to take out any internal dialogue that we don't need. There's no sense in spending time editing it if it will just end up cut in the end.

Step 1 – Compare your fast-paced action scenes to your slower-paced scenes. Are you using the same amount of internal dialogue in each? This should be easy to see since you've highlighted your passages of internal dialogue. If you are, work on trimming out any unnecessary internal dialogue in the scenes that are meant to be faster-paced.

Step 2 – Quickly check the beginning and ending paragraphs of each of your scenes. Are you forecasting? If so, delete it.

Step 3 – Check if you're using internal dialogue in almost every paragraph that focuses on your point-of-view character. This should be easy to see since you've already color-coded your passages. If you see that you have internal dialogue in almost every paragraph that focuses on your POV character, you're probably overusing internal dialogue. Try to reduce some of it by replacing it with other character reactions.

Step 4 – Copy and paste (in order) all the spots where your character is thinking about the same thing and make note of what page that selection came from. Read it over. This will quickly show you if there's progress in her thoughts or if she's basically running on a mouse wheel and getting nowhere.

Step 5 – Look at the passages where your character has a major revelation or takes a major emotional hit. Do they react to it? Is their reaction in proportion to whatever caused it?

Bonus Step – When you eventually ask a friend, critique partner, beta reader, or editor to read your manuscript, make sure to ask them to mark any spot where they aren't sure why your character is acting the way they are.

Chapter Four Exercises

Step 1 – For each section of internal dialogue, label it with either a C (for character), a P (for plot), or an S (for subtle element).

You can use the Comment feature within Microsoft Word to do this if you'd like (and if that's what you're using as your word processing program). Alternatively, you can work backward on this. If you can apply a label, don't leave a comment. If you can't, use the Comment feature to flag that passage for revision.

If you find that you can't apply one of those labels, you need to either remove or rewrite that section of internal dialogue.

Step 2 – For each passage of internal dialogue, ask yourself this question: Is this internal dialogue a reaction to what came before it?

If so, it can stay.

If not, you need to change it or rewrite it so that it does connect to what came before it.

Chapter Five Exercises

Look at the patterns created by your highlighting and color-coded text. Check for the following:

Step 1 – Does each passage of internal dialogue show up in a paragraph either by itself or focused on the point-of-view character?

Step 2 – Do you have long sections where you don't swap your focus often enough? This can indicate that you're either neglecting reactions by your character or that you're focusing on your POV character for too long at one time.

Chapter Seven Exercises

We've finally reached the fine-tuning part of our self-editing. We're going to deal with internal questions now and then move on to formatting.

Open the Advanced Find box and add a question mark. Click Find Next.

Along with showing you internal questions, this will show you questions in dialogue. You can skip those.

When you reach an internal dialogue question, ask yourself whether it does one of these things:

- Does it punctuate a character's emotions through (mostly) rhetorical questions?
- Does it show a character figuring something out or making an intuitive leap?
- Does it reinforce the scene or story goal, or serve as a reminder of what's at stake if the goal isn't reached?
- Does it show that your character is sarcastic in nature?
- Does it show an I'm-trying-to-convince-myself denial of what the character knows to be true or the character debating with themselves?
- Does it increase tension, conflict, or emotional upheaval?

If it doesn't do one of these things, odds are that you can safely remove it and that you won't lose anything.

For the questions that remain, ask yourself if there's a different way you could write it that would still clearly deliver the message or the same impact. If so, rewrite it.

Chapter Three Exercises

Skim through your internal dialogue and fix any formatting mistakes.

Microsoft Word provides a great quick trick if you notice you've italicized internal dialogue that you shouldn't have. Go to Find, and then choose Advanced Find. A box will pop up. Make sure your cursor is blinking in the "Find what:" box. Now, select Format and then Font. Select Italics and click OK. It will now take you to each italicized section just as if you were searching for a word.

Other Books by Marcy Kennedy

For Writers

Showing and Telling in Fiction

You've heard the advice "show, don't tell" until you can't stand to hear it anymore. Yet fiction writers of all levels still seem to struggle with it.

There are three reasons for this. The first is that this isn't an absolute rule. Telling isn't always wrong. The second is that we lack a clear way of understanding the difference between showing and telling. The third is that we're told "show, don't tell," but we're often left without practical ways to know how and when to do that, and how and when not to. So that's what this book is about.

Chapter One defines showing and telling and explains why showing is normally better.

Chapter Two gives you eight practical ways to find telling that needs to be changed to showing and guides you in understanding how to make those changes.

Chapter Three explains how telling can function as a useful first-draft tool.

Chapter Four goes in-depth on the seven situations when telling might be a better choice than showing.

Chapter Five provides you with practical editing tips to help you take what you've learned to the pages of your current novel or short story. *Showing and Telling in Fiction: A Busy Writer's Guide* also includes three appendices covering how to use *The Emotion Thesaurus*, dissecting an example so you can see the concepts of showing vs. telling in action, and explaining the closely related topic of As-You-Know-Bob Syndrome.

Dialogue

How do you properly format dialogue? How can you write dialogue unique to each of your characters? Is it okay to start a chapter with dialogue? Writers all agree that great dialogue helps make great fiction, but it's not as easy to write as it looks.

In *Dialogue: A Busy Writer's Guide*, you'll learn

- how to format your dialogue,
- how to add variety to your dialogue so it's not always "on the nose,"
- when you should use dialogue and when you shouldn't,
- how to convey information through dialogue without falling prey to As-You-Know-Bob Syndrome,
- how to write dialogue unique to each of your characters,
- how to add tension to your dialogue,
- whether it's ever okay to start a chapter with dialogue,
- ways to handle contractions (or a lack thereof) in science fiction, fantasy, and historical fiction,
- tricks for handling dialect,
- and much more!

Each book in the *Busy Writer's Guide* series is intended to give you enough theory so that you can understand why things work and why they don't, but also enough examples to see how that theory looks in practice. In addition, they provide tips and exercises to help you take it to the pages of your own story with an editor's-eye view.

Grammar for Fiction Writers

Not your same old boring grammar guide! This book is fun, fast, and focused on writing amazing fiction.

The world of grammar is huge, but fiction writers don't need to know all the nuances to write well. In fact, some of the rules you were taught in English class will actually hurt your fiction writing, not help it.

Grammar for Fiction Writers won't teach you things you don't need to know. It's all about the grammar that's relevant to you as you write your novels and short stories.

Here's what you'll find inside:

- **Punctuation Basics** including the special uses of dashes and ellipses in fiction, common comma problems, how to format your dialogue, and untangling possessives and contractions.

- **Knowing What Your Words Mean and What They Don't** including commonly confused words, imaginary words and phrases, how to catch and strengthen weak words, and using connotation and denotation to add powerful subtext to your writing.

- **Grammar Rules Every Writer Needs to Know and Follow** such as maintaining an active voice and making the best use of all the tenses for fast-paced writing that feels immediate and draws the reader in.

- **Special Challenges for Fiction Writers** like reversing cause and effect, characters who are unintentionally doing the impossible, and orphaned dialogue and pronouns.

- Grammar "Rules" You Can Safely Ignore When Writing Fiction

Twitter for Authors

Building a thriving social media platform doesn't have to steal all your precious writing time or cut into your time with your family. *Twitter for Authors: A Busy Writer's Guide* is about building a successful Twitter platform that's sustainable for busy people.

Twitter often gets a bad reputation from people who don't understand it or don't know how to use it to its full potential to build an author platform. When used correctly, Twitter can be one of the best tools for increasing traffic to your blog and gaining new readers for your books. And it's fun!

In *Twitter for Authors*, you'll learn...

- essential Twitter terminology,
- how to set up your account,
- the differences between TweetDeck and Hootsuite,
- techniques for staying safe on Twitter,
- how to build columns and lists and use them to find readers,
- the value of link shorteners and hashtags,
- what to tweet about,
- the most common mistakes writers make on Twitter,
- how to run a successful Twitter event,
- how to manage your social media time,
- and much more!

Twitter for Authors contains helpful advice for both Twitter newbies and long-time Twitter users who want to take their platform to the next level.

Fiction

Frozen: Two Suspenseful Short Stories

Twisted sleepwalking.

A frozen goldfish in a plastic bag.

And a woman afraid she's losing her grip on reality.

"A Purple Elephant" is a suspense short story about grief and betrayal.

In "The Replacements," a prodigal returns home to find that her parents have started a new family, one with no room for her. This disturbing suspense short story is about the lengths to which we'll go to feel like we're wanted, and how we don't always see things the way they really are.

ABOUT THE AUTHOR

Marcy Kennedy is a science fiction, fantasy, and suspense author, freelance editor, and writing instructor who believes there's always hope. Sometimes you just have to dig a little harder to find it. In a world that can be dark and brutal and unfair, hope is one of our most powerful weapons.

She writes novels that encourage people to keep fighting. She wants to let them know that no one is beyond redemption and that, in the end, good always wins.

She writes books for writers to give them the courage to keep writing. She wants to let them know that they can achieve their dream of creating fantastic stories if they're willing to work for it.

She's also a proud Canadian and the proud wife of a former U.S. Marine; owns four cats, two birds, and a dog who weighs as much as she does; and plays board games and the flute (not at the same time). Sadly, she's also addicted to coffee and jelly beans.

You can find her blogging at www.marcykennedy.com about writing and about the place where real life meets science fiction, fantasy, and myth. To sign up for her new-release mailing list, please go to the link below. Not only will you hear about new releases before anyone else, but you'll also receive exclusive discounts and freebies. Your email address will never be shared, and you can unsubscribe at any time.

Newsletter: http://eepurl.com/Bk2Or

Website: www.marcykennedy.com

Email: marcykennedy@gmail.com

Facebook: www.facebook.com/MarcyKennedyAuthor

Printed in Great Britain
by Amazon

69145159R00078